ISBN 978-1-5278-2269-6
PIBN 10893745

1 MONTH OF
FREE
READING

at
www.ForgottenBooks.com

By purchasing this book you are eligible for one month membership to ForgottenBooks.com, giving you unlimited access to our entire collection of over 1,000,000 titles via our web site and mobile apps.

To claim your free month visit:
www.forgottenbooks.com/free893745

Historic, archived document

Do not assume content reflects current
scientific knowledge, policies, or practices.

8946 **ROSE, PEACE.** *Plant Pat. 591.* $2.00 each

PORTER-WALTON'S

Book

P. O. Box 1619
Salt Lake City 11, Utah

for 1950

LAWN GRASS SEEDS

Clean—Dependable—Vigorous

ASK FOR FREE LEAFLET, "HOW TO BUILD AND MAINTAIN A BEAUTIFUL LAWN"

P.-W.'s "GREEN LAWN MIXTURES"

We are especially proud of these lawn mixtures. They are composed of pure seeds of those fine-leaved and deep-rooted permanent grasses best suited for residence lawns.

2970 Velvet Green. Sow 1 pound per 200 square feet. Most permanently beautiful and most easily maintained, this superior lawn mixture is the favorite among professional as well as amateur gardeners. Containing only Kentucky Blue Grass and White Dutch Clover, Velvet Green Mixture remains fine and velvety indefinitely; stays green from early spring until late fall.

2974 Evergreen. Sow 1 pound per 200 square feet. An exceptionally hardy grass mixture containing Kentucky Blue Grass, Creeping Red Fescue and White Dutch Clover. This blend is adapted to sunny or partially shaded areas; it will withstand rough usage and on light sandy soils is more drought resistant than straight Blue Grass.

2980 Shady Nook Mixture. Sow 1 pound per 200 square feet. A proved formula including varieties that are shade tolerant.

2988. ATHLETIC FIELD MIXTURE

Sow 1 pound per 150 square feet

This blend of grasses consisting of Kentucky Blue Grass, Meadow Fescue, and Perennial Rye Grass is especially adapted for athletic fields, playgrounds and park areas. It is very hardy and will withstand tramping and considerable hard usage. Adapted to planting in alkaline soil.

LAWN GRASSES

2966 Kentucky Blue Grass, Fancy Grade, Triple Cleaned (*Poa pratensis*). Sow 1 pound per 200 square feet. A deep green grass that does well on most types of soil. It continues to grow at low temperatures and keeps your lawn green in spring and autumn. Kentucky Blue is the backbone of fine lawn mixtures. It is aggressive and spreads rapidly, making a sod of fine texture.

LAWN GRASSES

2950 Astoria Bent Grass, Blue Tag Certified Grade. Sow 1 pound per 400 square feet. Properly cared for, Bent makes a beautiful lawn, discouraging weed growth. It is the true creeping type and forms a very dense sod.

2960 Creeping Red Fescue. Sow 1 pound per 150 square feet. Like Chewings Fescue, it is exceptional on sandy or gravelly soils and unexcelled in shade. The turfs of the finer strains of Red Fescue are probably the most beautiful of all lawn grasses.

2990 WHITE DUTCH CLOVER. For reseeding use 1 pound per 1000 square feet. The best Clover to include in grass mixtures. Its advantages are that it grows quickly, remains green all season, and is helpful to grasses growing with it. Gardeners who prefer heavy Clover growth should include 2 ounces to each pound of grass seed.

LAWN SEED PRICES

Quantity prices apply only when the quantity is of a single variety.

	Lb.	2-4 lbs. per lb.	5-9 lbs. per lb.	10-24 lbs. per lb.	25-99 lbs. per lb.	100 lbs. up per lb.
2970 Velvet Green Mix	$1 25	$1 20	$1 15	$1 08	$1 00	$0 91
2974 Evergreen Mix	1 10	1 05	1 00	95	90	82
2980 Shady Nook Mix	1 20	1 15	1 10	1 05	99	90
2988 Athletic Field Mix	55	50	49	46	43	39
2966 Kentucky Blue	1 20	1 15	1 10	1 05	97	89
2950 Astoria Bent	2 20	2 05	1 95	1 85	1 70	1 55
2960 Creeping Red Fescue	1 05	1 00	95	88	82	75
2990 White Dutch Clover	1 40	1 35	1 30	1 25	1 17	

PORTER-WALTON COMPANY

SEED

Save

It is
safer to b
in P.-W.'
ets and c
protect.
prevent
stored se
ready-pa
in your b

MOUNTAIN-GROWN SEEDS

Best for the West

The production of MOUNTAIN-GROWN SEEDS employs the most careful and scientific methods. Only seeds of the purest strains and of the highest purity and germination will produce the top-quality flowers and vegetables to which Mountain-Grown Seed planters are accustomed.

BUY THEM FROM YOUR LOCAL DEALER

Save Shopping Time

It is quicker and safer to buy your seeds in P.-W.'s sealed packets and cartons. They protect vitality and prevent mixing of stored seeds. Look for ready-packaged seeds in your local seed store.

SOLD IN GROCERY AND SUPPLY STORES OVER THE INTERMOUNTAIN WEST

SEED AND NURSERY SPECIALISTS

GROW THESE *All-America Selections*

27 BEAN, Topcrop

50 days. All-America Gold Medal winner and an important milepost in Bean breeding progress. Higher yields over a short harvest period and smooth, round, meaty, light green pods entirely without strings or fiber are characteristic of Topcrop. It is a more vigorous grower, highly resistant to Bean mosaic and is earlier than Tendergreen. In several years of testing it has proved to be widely adaptable and a very dependable, heavy cropper. Pkt. 20c; 1 to 4 lbs., 50c per lb.

525 SQUASH, Uconn

The All-America Selection for 1950. Uconn, this year's Gold Medal winner, is a bush form of the popular Acorn or Table Queen Squash. The small but very productive plants offer a distinct advantage for both home and commercial gardeners. A dual-purpose Squash—the first immature fruits can be boiled as summer Squash and the later ones left on the plant to mature for winter use. The deep green individual-size fruits have a rich meaty flavor and keep well for several months. Pkt. 20c; oz. 35c; lb. $3.50.

173 CORN, Stowell's Evergreen Hybrid

90 days. Bronze Medal, 1934. A white hybrid Corn adapted to home or market garden and for freezing or canning. The tender, sweet kernels are deep, medium wide and set in 14 to 18 rows on thick ears about 8 inches long. Like its parent, it is a tall grower but has greater uniformity of maturity. Pkt. 20c; 1 to 4 lbs., 55c per lb.

451 RADISH, Cherry Belle

Bronze Medal, 1949. Here is a delightfully tasty and tangy Radish with the brightest red color of all. The globes are perfectly round and the flesh fine grained, crisp and firm at all stages. Cherry Belle has short tops, makes attractive bunches for market use and does not become pithy. It is excellent for spring and fall gardens and holds its own in summer plantings. Pkt. 10c; oz. 20c; ¼lb. 50c; 1 to 4 lbs., $1.45 per lb; 5 to 24 lbs., $1.35 per lb.

451 RADISH, CHERRY BELLE

525 SQUASH, UCONN

173 CORN, STOWELL'S EVERGREEN HYBRID

27 BEANS, TOPCROP

COLLECTION No. 589

ONE PACKET each of these four outstanding vegetables enough for a home garden planting.
(*A 70c value*) . . . . ONLY **60¢**

4

PORTER-WALTON COMPANY

Mountain-Grown VEGETABLE SEEDS

ASPARAGUS SEED
An ounce of seed will sow 75 feet of row and produce about 250 plants

Sow the seed in early spring. Set the plants 18 inches apart, with 3 feet between the rows. Given care, a bed of 500 square feet supplies an average family for eight to ten years.

10 **Mary Washington.** An early, rust-resistant variety that is a very heavy producer. Pkt. 10c; oz. 20c; ¼lb. 60c; 1 to 4 lbs., $1.75 per lb.; 5 to 24 lbs., $1.57 per lb.

12 **New Paradise.** Produces a normal crop one year earlier. Heavy cropper; finest quality. Pkt. 10c; oz. 40c; ¼lb. $1.25; lb. $3.75.
For roots, see page 12.

STRINGLESS BEANS
Dwarf Greenpod Beans
A packet will plant 30 feet, a pound 150 feet, 60 to 75 pounds an acre

30 **Tendergreen** or **P.-W.'s Stringless Greenpod.** 55 days. The leading stringless green-pod sort. Pods are 6 to 6½ inches long, absolutely stringless and free from fiber. Pkt. 20c; 1 to 4 lbs., 45c per lb.

27 **Topcrop.** All-America Bean for 1950. See page 4.

32 **Landreth's Stringless Greenpod.** 53 days. Replaces Burpee's Stringless. The pods of this excellent green Bean are stringless, fiberless, straight, and 6 to 6½ inches long. Pkt. 20c; 1 to 4 lbs., 45c per lb.

Dwarf Wax-Pod Beans
Sow at the same rate as Greenpod varieties

35 **Puregold Wax.** 59 days. Here at last is a Wax Bean that possesses both high quality and high productivity. The dwarf bushes produce long, slim, round pods of clear buttery gold. Its quality is far superior to Pencil-Pod, and the white seeds add a clean freshness to its appearance when canned or frozen. Resistant to common Bean mosaic. Best freezing variety. Pkt. 20c; 1 to 4 lbs., 45c per lb.

36 **Pencil-Pod Black Wax.** 58 days. Six to 7 inches in length, of a rich golden yellow color. Our stocks are carefully selected and uniform. Pkt. 20c; 1 to 4 lbs., 45c per lb.

Pole Beans
A packet will plant 120 feet of row

40 **Blue Lakes Stringless** (White Seeded). Used extensively by intermountain and Pacific Coast canners for an asparagus type pack of green Beans. Splendid for home use. Good climber and heavy producer. Very fleshy, brittle, and tender.

44 **Kentucky Wonder or Homestead.** 65 days. The pods are thick, meaty and entirely stringless. The best for all purposes.

All Pole Beans, pkt. 20c; 1 to 4 lbs., 45c per lb.

QUANTITY PRICES
f.o.b. Salt Lake City
Add postage at zone rates

	5 to 9 lbs. per lb.	10 to 24 lbs. per lb.	25 to 99 lbs. per lb.	Bag Lots, 100 lbs.
Tendergreen	$0 36	$0 33	$0 30	$28 00
Topcrop	41	38	35	33 00
Landreth's Stringless Greenpod	32	29	26	24 00
Puregold Wax	39	36	33	31 50
Pencil-Pod Black Wax	38	35	32	30 00
Pole, Blue Lakes Stringless	39	36	33	31 00
Pole, Kentucky Wonder	36	33	30	28 00

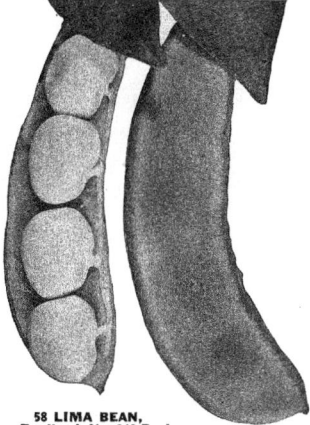

58 LIMA BEAN, Fordhook No. 242 Bush

LIMA BEANS, Bush and Pole
A pound will plant 100 feet of row, about 60 pounds an acre.

58 **Fordhook No. 242 Bush.** 72 days. An improved strain of Fordhook, which outyields its parent by a three-to-two ratio. The outstanding characteristic of 242 is its ability to set seed at high temperatures. Excellent quality. Good freezer. Pkt. 30c; 1 to 4 lbs., 55c per lb.

60 **Henderson Bush** (Baby Lima). 65 days. An early, productive sort. Pods about 2¾ inches long. Pkt. 20c; 1 to 4 lbs., 45c per lb.

62 **King of the Garden** (Pole Lima). 88 days. The Beans are oval and plump, pale green at the tender stage and greenish white when mature. Very productive. Pkt. 30c; 1 to 4 lbs., 55c per lb.

BROAD WINDSOR BEANS

50 **Long-Pod Fava.** An improved variety having long pods with 4 to 5 large, flat Beans. Very hardy; should be planted as soon as the ground can be worked in the spring. Pkt. 20c; 1 to 4 lbs., 45c per lb.

QUANTITY PRICES
f.o.b. Salt Lake City

	5 to 9 lbs. per lb.	10 to 24 lbs. per lb.	25 to 99 lbs. per lb.	Bag Lots, 100 lbs.
Fordhook No. 242 Bush Lima	$0 45	$0 42	$0 39	$37 50
Henderson Bush Lima	32	29	26	24 00
King of the Garden (Pole Lima)	41	38	35	33 00
Long-Pod Fava	32	29	26	24 00

SHIPPING WEIGHTS
Although all stock in this catalog is priced f.o.b. Salt Lake City, the weight of vegetable seeds in packets and ounces need not be included with shipping weights for postage. Include weights for postage on each item of ¼ pound or more.

80 BEET, Detroit Dark Red

BEETS

An ounce will sow 60 feet of row, a packet 15 feet, 10 pounds an acre in rows spaced 14 inches apart

80 **Detroit Dark Red** (Perfected Strain). The most outstanding selection of Detroit Dark Red for dark, uniform interior color. The root is globe shaped, slightly flattened at base. Especially adaptable for market gardens or canning. Tops are fairly large.

82 **Early Blood** (Dark Red Strain). 50 to 55 days. An extra-early variety, splendid for home gardens or markets. Roots are globe shaped, very dark red, with medium-sized tops.

85 **Green-Top Bunching.** 50 to 55 days. An early Beet with medium-sized, erect, grayish green, fresh-looking tops. The roots, 2½ to 3 inches in diameter, are round, smooth, glossy, selling readily in the markets. The flesh is bright blood-red, of finer texture and with less fiber than most bunching Beets.

All Beets, pkt. 10c; oz. 20c; ¼lb. 50c; 1 to 4 lbs., $1.25 per lb.; 5 to 24 lbs., $1.20 per lb.

BROCCOLI

90 **Italian Green Sprouting.** 80 days. Cultivated like cabbage, it produces a large central head followed by a succession of side sprouts. Each sprout, about 4 inches long, ends in a small head of deep green buds. They resemble miniature cauliflower heads except in color. Pkt. 10c; oz. 35c; ¼lb. $1.00; lb. $3.00.

BRUSSELS SPROUTS

94 **Long Island Improved.** The flavor of these small sprouts or heads is more delicate than that of cabbage. Firm, round, cabbage-like balls about 1¾ inches in diameter mature in succession. Pkt. 10c; oz. 55c; ¼lb. $1.65; lb. $5.00.

CHICORY

162 **Large Rooted or Coffee.** The roots when dried are used as a coffee substitute. The young leaves may be used in salad. Sow seeds early in spring in rows about 2 feet apart. Pkt. 10c; oz. 35c; ¼lb. $1.15; lb. $3.50.

CRESS

½ ounce will plant 100 feet of row

218 **Extra Curled or Pepper Grass.** Adds an excellent flavor to salads. Pkt. 10c; oz. 15c; ¼lb. 30c; 1 to 4 lbs., 95c per lb.

6

P.-W.'s SPECIAL CABBAGE STRAINS

An ounce will produce about 3,000 plan ts if sown in frames.

100 **Copenhagen Market.** 70 days. This fine early market-garden strain will satisfy the most critical trade. Good yielder and an excellent keeper.

102 **Danish Ballhead** (Short-Stem Strain). 110 days. We are proud of this stock and fully recommend it to our customers as the most outstanding Danish Ballhead offered anywhere. It is vigorous, uniform, and sure to head. Outstanding keeper in storage.

103 **Danish Keeping.** The longest-keeping Cabbage. The heads are extraordinarily solid. Although it grows slightly smaller than Danish Ballhead, it is more solid and heavier. A medium-stemmed Cabbage of late maturity and uniform quality. Pkt. 10c; oz. 35c; ¼lb. $1.10; 1 to 4 lbs., $3.25 per lb.

107 **Green Acre.** 65 days. A little larger than Golden Acre, making about 20 per cent more tonnage. Large, smooth leaves, dark green in color. Especially valuable to market gardeners and shippers. Pkt. 10c; oz. 35c; ¼lb. 95c; 1 to 4 lbs., $2.75 per lb.; 5 to 24 lbs., $2.60 per lb.

112 **Perfection Drumhead.** 90 days. The leading Savoy type Cabbage.

114 **Red Stonehead.** 110 days. The largest and best red Cabbage. Pkt. 10c; oz. 40c; ¼lb. $1.10; 1 to 4 lbs., $3.30 per lb.

All Cabbage, except where noted, pkt. 10c; oz. 30c; ¼lb. 90c; 1 to 4 lbs., $2.50 per lb.; 5 to 24 lbs., $2.35 per lb.

CHINESE CABBAGE

117 **Chihili.** Very dependable in heading. The heads are 18 to 20 inches long, compact and pointed at the top. Especially delicious as a salad. Pkt. 10c; oz. 20c; ¼lb. 60c; 1 to 4 lbs., $1.80 per lb.; 5 to 24 lbs., $1.60 per lb.

CARROTS

122 **Chantenay Red Cored.** 70 days. The flesh and core are reddish orange, fine grained, and tender.

124 **Nantes** (Coreless). 68 days. Very attractive, 6 to 7 inches long, smooth, cylindrical. Entirely coreless and exceptionally fine quality. Pkt. 10c; oz. 25c; ¼lb. 75c; 1 to 4 lbs., $2.10 per lb.; 5 to 24 lbs., $2.00 per lb.

126 **Imperator.** 77 days. Smooth, somewhat tapering, and deep orange in color.

128 **Danvers Red Cored.** An improved strain with superior dark red interior color. Outside is smoother, brighter and more attractive.

All Carrots, except where noted, pkt. 10c; oz. 20c; ¼lb. 60c; 1 to 4 lbs., $1.80 per lb.; 5 to 24 lbs., $1.60 per lb.

107 CABBAGE, Green Acre

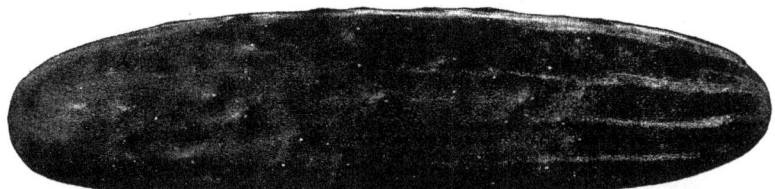

207 CUCUMBER, Marketer

CAULIFLOWER

An ounce will produce 1,500 to 2,000 plants in open ground or about 3,000 in frames

140 **P.-W.'s Perfection** (Super Snowball). 60 days. Most dependable of the early Snowball strains. It is adapted for either early or late fall use. The leaves are longer and fold closely over the heads, bleaching them nicely.

142 **New Snowdrift.** 67 days. Also known as White Mountain and Improved Holland Erfurt. Will produce a more satisfactory yield under extreme weather conditions than any other Snowball strain we know. The heads are somewhat larger than the old type Snowball, and it matures over a longer harvest period.

All Cauliflower, pkt. 10c; ½oz. $1.50; oz. $2.75; ¼lb. $9.00; lb. $27.50

UTAH CELERY
Famous from Coast to Coast

An ounce will produce about 1,500 plants; ½ pound will transplant an acre

150 **P.-W.'s IMPROVED UTAH.** 125 days. This is the far-famed Utah Celery so much in demand, which was developed by local gardeners. Its superior qualities are recognized everywhere, and many carloads, as well as thousands of personalized gift packages, are distributed to every part of the nation. It has double the amount of heart of any other Celery. The plant is compact and blanches to creamy white. The ribs are perfectly solid and crisp. Our true strain produces the most uniform, large, compact plants of any stocks produced in Utah. Pkt. 10c; ½oz. 85c; oz. $1.50; ¼lb. $4.00; lb. $11.00.

CELERIAC · Turnip-Rooted Celery

156 **Giant Smooth Prague.** This vegetable should be in every home garden. The bulbs are delicious when cut into cubes, boiled and served with a cream sauce. Pkt. 10c; oz. 65c; ¼lb. $2.00; lb. $6.00.

150 CELERY, P.-W.'S Improved Utah

◞ SEED AND NURSERY SPECIALISTS

CUCUMBER

A packet will plant 20 hills, an ounce 75 hills, 2 to 3 pounds an acre

207 **Marketer.** Now the leading market-garden variety. The fruits are from 7½ to 8 inches long and 2¼ inches in diameter. The flesh is crisp, icy-white in color, with a small seed cavity. Marketer is one of the most prolific varieties in existence, and its uniform shape and attractive color make it a profitable one to grow. Pkt. 10c; oz. 30c; ¼lb. 75c; 1 to 4 lbs. $2.25 per lb.

202 **Boston Pickling.** Very productive; extensively grown for pickles. Very smooth and symmetrical; flesh crisp and tender. Pkt. 10c; oz. 25c; ¼lb. 65c; 1 to 4 lbs., $1.80 per lb.

203 **Colorado.** 60 days. Popular because of its fine shape and uniform color, which is maintained longer than that of most varieties. A heavy yielder. Pkt. 10c; oz. 30c; ¼lb. 75c; 1 to 4 lbs., $2.10 per lb.

206 **Improved Long Green.** 62 days. Very vigorous and productive. Fruits long, uniformly slender, beautiful dark green. The stock we offer is second to none. Pkt. 10c; oz. 25c; ¼lb. 65c; 1 to 4 lbs., $1.80 per lb.

COLLARDS

216 **Georgia Southern or Creole.** This is a tall, loose-leaved, cabbage-like plant. Sow seed early in rows and transplant or thin to 4 inches in the row. Pkt. 10c; oz. 15c; ¼lb. 30c; 1 to 4 lbs., 95c per lb.

DILL See Herbs, below.

HERBS, Aromatic and Sweet

240 **ANISE.** 15 in. Seeds and leaves for flavoring.

242 **CARAWAY.** 15 in. Seed used to flavor breads, etc.

244 **CATNIP.** 20 in. Leaves used for flavoring.

245 **CORIANDER.** 30 in. Seed used in bread and confectionery.

246 **DILL.** 36 in. Seed used in soups and stews. Most used in pickling. Pkt. 10c; oz. 15c; ¼lb. 45c; lb. $1.25.

248 **FENNEL.** Stems for salads; seeds flavor candy.

250 **HOREHOUND.** Foliage and roots used for flavoring.

480 **SAGE** (*Salvia officinalis*). Much in demand for seasoning. Pkt. 10c; ½oz. 40c; oz. 65c; ¼lb. $2.00. For plants, see page 12.

252 **SWEET MARJORAM.** 24 in. Used for salads and dressings.

254 **SUMMER SAVORY.** 12 in. Leaves flavor salads, dressings, etc.

All Herbs, except where noted, pkt. 10c.

EGGPLANT

An ounce will produce 1,000 plants

220 **Black Beauty.** Earliest and best of all large-fruited Eggplants. The fruits are thick, uniform in shape, and most attractive in color. Pkt. 10c; ½oz. 50c; oz. 80c; ¼lb. $2.50; lb. $7.00.

7

SWEET CORN

A pound will plant about 400 hills, a packet 100 hills, 12 pounds an acre

Plant Hybrid Sweet Corn for Greater Productivity. Greater Drought and Pest Resistance

174 SWEET CORN, Golden Cross Bantam

Hybrid Varieties

178 **Spancross.** 70 to 73 days. One of the earliest hybrids. Produces medium-sized ears with 10 to 12 rows of medium-depth kernels of good flavor and quality.

170 **Marcross C6.13.** The leading early hybrid (74 to 77 days.) The 5-foot stalks produce 8-inch, 10 to 14-rowed, golden yellow ears well filled to the tip. Inherently disease-and drought-resistant, it is highly productive and dependable. Usually over 85 per cent of the ears are marketable.

176 **Ioana.** Midseason (86 days). Large-eared, wilt-resistant hybrid. The ears are slightly tapering, mostly 8 to 9 inches long, with 12 to 14 rows of creamy yellow, medium-deep kernels, which fill the ear well to the tip. These ears are of fine quality, sweet and tender.

174 **Golden Cross Bantam.** 93 to 95 days. The most prolific yellow Sweet Corn; produces at least 40 per cent more good marketable ears than ordinary stocks. The plant is sturdy, with broad, dark green leaves.

173 **Stowell's Hybrid** (White). See page 4.

175 **Everbearing Blend.** A single planting produces edible ears over a period of 4 to 5 weeks. Especially blended for home gardeners.

All Hybrid Sweet Corn, pkt. 20c; 1 to 4 lbs., 55c per lb.

Open-Pollinated Varieties

180 **Golden Bantam** (True 8-row Stock). 72 days. Broad, golden kernels of most delicious flavor.

186 **Golden Sunshine.** 65 days. Medium long and plump, with fine-quality kernels.

188 **Stowell's Evergreen.** 98 days. The best-known late white variety.

All Open-Pollinated Corn, pkt. 20c; 1 to 4 lbs., 35c per lb.

QUANTITY PRICES

f.o.b. Salt Lake City
These rates apply to large quantities of one variety

	5 to 9 lbs. per lb.	10 to 24 lbs. per lb.	25 to 99 lbs. per lb.	Bag Lots, 100 lbs.
Marcross	$0 43	$0 40	$0 37	$35 00
Spancross	43	40	37	35 00
Stowell's Hybrid	43	40	37	35 00
All other Hybrid Sweet Corn	38	35	32	30 00
Golden Sunshine	25	22	19	18 00
Stowell's Evergreen	26	23	20	18 50
Golden Bantam	25	22	19	17 50
Improved Bantam	25	22	19	17 50
Golden Rod	25	22	19	17 50

ENDIVE

An ounce will plant 300 feet, 4 to 5 pounds an acre

A salad vegetable valuable for winter use. Sow in rows in June or July, and thin to about six inches.

226 **Broad-Leaved Batavian.** Broad, more or less twisted and waved green leaves with thick white midribs.

228 **Green Curled.** Midribs are wide and whitish, with the outer edges very much indented.

All Endive, pkt. 10c; oz. 20c; ¼ lb. 55c; 1 to 4 lbs., $1.60 per lb.; 5 to 24 lbs., $1.40 per lb.

KALE

A packet will plant 100 feet, 2 pounds an acre

260 **Dwarf Curled Scotch.** A species of cabbage. The leaves are cooked as greens. Grows very low and compact. Pkt. 10c; oz. 25c; ¼ lb. 75c; lb. $2.25.

KOHLRABI

An ounce will plant 300 feet of row

266 **Early White Vienna.** Very early, with small tops. Roots medium size and best quality. Pkt. 10c; oz. 35c; ¼ lb. $1.15; lb. $3.50.

PORTER-WALTON COMPANY

272 LETTUCE, Great Lakes

LETTUCE

272 Great Lakes. Being very resistant to tip-burn, able to withstand heat and sun, and remarkably slow to throw a seed-head, Great Lakes is one of the most popular summer Lettuces. Pkt. 10c; ½oz. 35c; oz. 50c; ¼lb. $1.65; 1 to 4 lbs., $5.00 per lb.; 5 to 24 lbs., $4.50 per lb.

274 Imperial No. 847. Especially fine for late spring and summer. It is a black-seeded variety that shows remarkable resistance to heat. Large, firm heads, dark green and of high quality. Pkt. 10c; ½oz. 20c; oz. 35c; ¼lb. $1.10; 1 to 4 lbs., $3.20 per lb.; 5 to 24 lbs., $3.00 per lb.

276 Imperial No. 44. Surest-heading Iceberg Lettuce. This outstanding Lettuce does well on a wide range of soils, both upland and muck but especially muck. Not only does it head better than any other strain, but it has shown definite resistance to tip-burn. Pkt. 10c; ½oz. 20c; oz. 35c; ¼lb. $1.10; 1 to 4 lbs., $3.20 per lb.; 5 to 24 lbs., $3.00 per lb.

279 Pennlake. Winner of the All-America Selections Bronze Medal for 1949. Very strongly resistant to heat and tip-burn, Pennlake makes a well-formed, solid head. Lacking the prominent midribs of its parent, Great Lakes, it is more refined in appearance and texture. About the same season as Great Lakes. Pkt. 10c; ½oz. 35c; oz. 55c; ¼lb. $2.00; 1 to 4 lbs., $6.00 per lb.; 5 to 24 lbs., $5.75 per lb.

271 Premier Great Lakes. This improved new strain produces heads from 7 to 10 days earlier than standard Great Lakes. Yields up to 90 per cent marketable heads, each unusually solid, up to 7 inches in diameter and 2 pounds in weight. Other advantages are slow bolting habit and high resistance to heat. Pkt. 10c; ½oz. 35c; oz. 55c; ¼lb. $1.80; lb. $5.60.

Loose-Leaf Lettuce

286 Early Curled Simpson. 45 days. A popular early sort, forming a large, loose head.

288 Prizehead. 47 days. Large, loose-headed sort; very thick leaves tinged with brown.

All Loose-Leaf Lettuce, pkt. 10c; oz. 20c; ¼lb. 70c; lb. $2.00

LEEK

Seed should be planted in June for good plants in fall or winter.

270 Emperor. The best variety, having good thick stems which are long, vigorous and mild flavored. Pkt. 10c; ½oz. 35c; oz. 60c; ¼lb. $1.75; lb. $5.00.

MANGELS

See page 57

SEED AND NURSERY SPECIALISTS

MUSTARD

An ounce will plant 50 feet of row

294 Giant Southern Curled. Excellent greens, cooked like spinach. Large curled leaves with pleasing mild flavor. Pkt. 10c; oz. 15c; ¼lb. 25c; lb. 75c.

MUSKMELONS OR CANTALOUPES

310 Jumbo Hale's Best. 90 days. For roadside markets and home gardens where a larger melon is desirable, this variety is unsurpassed. It is one-third larger than the older No. 936, attaining 8 inches in diameter.

304 Resistant No. 45. 86 days. Size 6 x 5½ inches; weight about 4 pounds. Small seed cavity; thick, deep-colored flesh of delicious flavor. This mildew-resistant H.B. type melon surpasses all others for shipping to distant markets. The flesh remains firm and edible for 10 days or longer after picking.

306 Honey Dew. 110 days. Excellent for roadside stands because of attractive color and thick flesh with honey-like flavor. Golden rind and green flesh. Fruits are round, smooth and solid, suitable for long-distance shipping.

308 Hearts of Gold Improved. 88 days. Fine for shipping as well as for general purposes. Medium size, round, and well netted. Firm orange-yellow flesh of excellent flavor, holding up well.

315 CRANSHAW. 110 days. A new hybrid melon of exceptional merit. For the home garden or local market its rich spicy flavor is especially prized. The flesh is bright salmon and very thick; fruits weigh 7 to 8 pounds each. They are pointed at the stem end and round at the base, with a relatively smooth skin mottled green and gold. The vigorous plants are very productive.

All Muskmelons, pkt. 10c; oz. 25c; ¼lb. 75c; 1 to 4 lbs., $2.00 per lb.; 5 to 24 lbs., $1.85 per lb.

Casaba Melons

300 Golden Beauty. 105 days. Most popular of the Casabas. Bright golden color, with deeply wrinkled skin when mature. Pkt. 10c; oz. 25c; ¼lb. 75c; 1 to 4 lbs., $2.00 per lb.; 5 to 24 lbs., $1.85 per lb.

OKRA OR GUMBO

A packet will plant 15 feet of row, an ounce 50 feet

342 Clemson Spineless. 55 days. An improved Perkins Long-podded type. Awarded All-America Silver Medal in 1939. A very uniform, spineless strain; straight pods of rich green. Pkt. 10c; oz. 15c; ¼lb. 35c; 1 to 4 lbs., $1.00 per lb.

PARSLEY

An ounce will plant 150 feet of row, 3 to 4 pounds an acre

402 Champion Moss Curled. A vigorous, compact sort with deep green, attractive foliage. One of the best for market or home use. Pkt. 10c; oz. 15c; ¼lb. 45c; 1 to 4 lbs., $1.25 per lb.

PARSNIPS

An ounce will plant 100 feet of row, 5 to 6 pounds an acre

410 New Harris White Model. Considered by all market gardeners who have tried it to be an improvement over Hollow Crown. It is of medium length, smooth, and is pure creamy white. The absence of side roots and the ease with which it is harvested are important points in its favor. Pkt. 10c; oz. 15c; ¼lb. 40c; 1 to 4 lbs., $1.25 per lb.

ONIONS

A packet will plant about 25 feet of row, ½ ounce 100 feet,
3 to 6 pounds an acre

For Bunch Onions sow 15 to 20 pounds per acre; for Sets,
about 50 pounds per acre

350 **Sweet Spanish.** (Utah Strain.) 110 days. Universally recognized for its excellence. Its superiority lies in its deep yellow color, large size, and remarkable uniformity. The firm white flesh is crisp, mild and tasty. Pkt. 10c; ½oz. 35c; oz. 50c; ¼lb. $1.65; 1 to 4 lbs., $5.00 per lb.; 5 to 24 lbs., $4.75 per lb.

352 **Certified Sweet Spanish.** (Utah Grown.) Onions at their best. One of Utah's major crops, produced from this superior strain. State sealed in one pound bags and larger. 1 to 4 lbs., $8.00 per lb.; 5 to 24 lbs., $7.50 per lb.

358 **Crystal White Wax.** A medium-large white Onion of the Bermuda type. Famous for its sweet, mild flavor. Our stock of this variety is imported from the finest source available. Pkt. 10c; ½oz. 30c; oz. 50c; ¼lb. $1.50; 1 to 4 lbs., $4.15 per lb.; 5 to 24 lbs., $4.00 per lb.

360 **Southport White Globe.** A fine white Onion. The solid, round bulbs are medium large and pure white. The flesh is waxy, fine grained, and mild. Keeps well in fall storage. Pkt. 10c; ½oz. 30c; oz. 50c; ¼lb. $1.50; 1 to 4 lbs., $4.50 per lb.; 5 to 24 lbs., $4.25 per lb.

362 **P.-W.'s White Sweet Spanish.** (Utah Jumbo Strain.) Similar in shape and habit of growth to P.-W.'s Sweet Spanish Onion. It has a beautiful white skin which makes it desirable for market. The flavor is unusually sweet and mild. A heavy yielder. Pkt. 10c; ½oz. 40c; oz. 65c; ¼lb. $2.00; 1 to 4 lbs., $6.00 per lb.; 5 to 24 lbs., $5.70 per lb.

372 **White Portugal or Silverskin.** An all-purpose variety used in great quantity. Excellent for sets, pickling or green bunching. A dependable cropper. Pkt. 10c; ½oz. 25c; oz. 40c; ¼lb. $1.25; 1 to 4 lbs., $3.75 per lb.; 5 to 24 lbs., $3.50 per lb.

373 **White Lisbon.** Grown almost exclusively as an early bunching Onion. It is round, with a thick neck and tender white flesh. If thinned and allowed to mature, the bulbs will reach almost 3 inches in diameter. Pkt. 10c; ½oz. 25c; oz. 40c; ¼lb. $1.25; 1 to 4 lbs., $3.75 per lb.; 5 to 24 lbs., $3.50 per lb.

Onion Sets

A quart (1 pound) will set 75 to 100 feet of row

Onions grown from sets mature 3 to 4 weeks earlier than those grown from seed.

376 **Yellow Sets.**
378 **White Sets.**

All Onion Sets, 1 to 4 lbs., 35c per lb.; 5 to 24 lbs., 27c per lb.

If by mail, add postage at zone rate.

PUMPKINS

An ounce will plant 20 hills, 3 pounds an acre

412 **Connecticut Field** (Big Tom). Large, orange-colored fruits, flat on the ends, with smooth, hard rind. For canning or pies; also used largely for stock feed.

418 **Sugar Pie.** A handsome and productive small Pumpkin, 10 to 12 inches in diameter; flat-round, with orange skin. Flesh deep yellow, of fine grain and very sweet.

All Pumpkins, pkt. 10c; oz. 20c; ¼lb. 55c; 1 to 4 lbs., $1.50 per lb.; 5 to 24 lbs., $1.35 per lb.

10

350 ONIONS, Sweet Spanish

PEAS

A packet will plant about 20 feet of row, a pound 100 feet,
100 to 200 pounds an acre

386 **Giant Stride** (Wilt Resistant). 75 days. The largest-podded variety of commercial importance. Especially adapted for the market gardener and shipper. The pods are 5½ inches long, dark green and plump. Giant Stride is an excellent variety for cold storage.

390 **Laxton's Progress.** 63 days. Produces the largest pods of any of the early dwarf varieties. Popular for long-distance shipping, also for home and market gardeners. We offer a very superior strain of this leading variety. Ordinarily two pickings will clean the vines. Vines 18 inches tall; pods 4½ to 5 inches long.

392 **Little Marvel.** 62 days. An outstanding early dwarf Pea for home gardens. Vigorous vines 18 inches tall, heavily laden with blunt, 3-inch pods. Very attractive Peas esteemed for their high table quality; fairly large at eating stage.

396 **Stratagem Improved.** 80 days. Fine late variety for home gardens, market growers, long-distance shippers. Vines 24 inches tall; 4½-inch, dark green pods. A very fine variety and a heavy yielder.

398 **Victory Freezer.** 65 days. This outstanding new All-America Selection is best adapted to home freezing or locker storage. It has the high productivity of Thomas Laxton but the Peas do not lose their skin in freezing. Medium sized, dark green, delicious in flavor, tender all the way through, and apparently skinless. Its greatly improved heat resistance allows wider garden use. The wilt-resistant vines are medium heavy, about 28 inches tall, producing 3 to 3½-inch pods in pairs instead of singly.

Each of above, pkt. 20c; 1 to 4 lbs. of one variety, 35c per lb.

QUANTITY PRICES

f.o.b. Salt Lake City

Quantity rates are allowed only on orders for 5 or more pounds of a single variety. When ordering several varieties, the price must be calculated separately for each variety ordered.

	5 to 9 lbs. per lb.	10 to 24 lbs. per lb.	25 to 99 lbs. per lb.	Bag Lots, 100 lbs.
Giant Stride	$0 29	$0 26	$0 23	$21 50
Laxton's Progress	31	28	25	23 00
Little Marvel	28	25	22	20 00
Stratagem Improved	29	26	23	21 50
Victory Freezer	30	27	24	22 00

PORTER-WALTON COMPANY

PEPPERS

An ounce will produce 1,000 plants

420 California Wonder, XXX Strain. Has all the qualities desired in a stuffing Pepper. Grows 4 inches in length and 3½ inches in diameter. A fine, sweet, tender Pepper with very thick walls. Smooth, glossy green fruits, changing to crimson when ripe. Pkt. 10c; ½oz. 55c; oz. 80c; ¼lb. $2.75; lb. $7.50.

428 Anaheim Chili. A hot late variety, popular because of its agreeable pungency. Fruits are 6 to 8 inches long, 1 inch wide, tapered. Pkt. 10c; ½oz. 45c; oz. 75c; ¼lb. $2.00; lb. $5.00.

430 Long Red Cayenne. Strong and pungent. Fruits about 5 inches long and ¾ inch thick. Pkt. 10c; ½oz. 45c; oz. 75c; ¼lb. $2.00; lb. $5.00.

436 Red Chili. Small, bright red, hot and pungent. About 2 inches long and ¼ to ½ inch thick. Pkt. 10c; ½oz. 45c; oz. 75c; ¼lb. $2.50; lb. $6.75.

RADISHES

An ounce will plant 50 feet of row, 3 to 4 pounds an acre

450 Comet (Long-standing). A medium-large, bright scarlet Radish of fine quality. It is globe shaped and lasts a long time without becoming pithy. Pkt. 10c; oz. 15c; ¼lb. 40c; 1 to 4 lbs., 95c per lb.; 5 to 24 lbs., 85c per lb.

451 Cherry Belle. See page 4.

452 P.-W.'s Sparkler. Round; brilliant scarlet with white base. Ready for the table in 20 days from planting. Pkt. 10c; oz. 15c; ¼lb. 40c; 1 to 4 lbs., 85c per lb.; 5 to 24 lbs., 80c per lb.

455 Cavalier. Because of its medium top growth in hot weather, Cavalier is the best of the Scarlet Globe types for summer planting. It matures quickly, with uniform, olive-shaped roots of brilliant scarlet. Pkt. 10c; oz. 15c; ¼lb. 40c; 1 to 4 lbs., 95c per lb.; 5 to 24 lbs., 85c per lb.

456 French Breakfast. 24 days. Medium-sized, olive-shaped roots, scarlet with white tip. Pkt. 10c; oz. 15c; ¼lb. 40c; 1 to 4 lbs., 85c per lb.; 5 to 24 lbs., 80c per lb.

458 Early Scarlet Globe (Medium Top). The principal variety used by commercial growers for early spring planting. Richly scarlet color; tender, mild and crisp. Bred for uniformity of slightly oval globes. Pkt. 10c; oz. 15c; ¼lb. 40c; 1 to 4 lbs., 85c per lb.; 5 to 24 lbs., 80c per lb.

460 Icicle. 27 days. Pure white, slender and tapering. The flesh is crisp and of splendid flavor. Pkt. 10c; oz. 15c; ¼lb. 40c; 1 to 4 lbs., 85c per lb.; 5 to 24 lbs., 80c per lb.

Winter Varieties

Seed for Winter Radishes should be sown about the first of August. For winter use the roots should be pulled and packed in damp sand stored in a cool cellar.

466 Celestial or White Chinese. Pure white, firm. Pkt. 10c; oz. 15c; ¼lb. 45c; lb. $1.25.

SALSIFY

Cultivate the same as carrots. Roots can remain in the ground all winter for early spring use.

486 Mammoth Sandwich Island. Grows to a very large size and resembles a good-sized parsnip. Mild and delicately flavored. Pkt. 10c; oz. 55c; ¼lb. $1.50; lb. $4.50.

SPINACH

¼ pound will plant 200 feet of row, 12 to 20 pounds an acre

490 Bloomsdale Long-Standing Improved (Savoy-leaved). We offer a wonderfully well-bred strain. Large, deep green, well-crumpled leaves, which produce enormous crops and stand a long time without bolting to seed. Pkt. 10c; oz. 15c; ¼lb. 30c; 1 to 4 lbs., 55c per lb.; 5 to 24 lbs., 50c per lb.; 25 to 99 lbs., 47c per lb.; 100 lbs. $45.00.

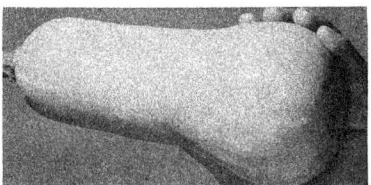

519 SQUASH, Butternut

SQUASH
Winter Varieties

¼ pound will plant 50 hills, 3 to 4 pounds an acre

514 Banana (Pink.) 120 days. Popular Winter Squash. Flesh fine grained, deep yellow, of excellent flavor. Pkt. 10c; oz. 25c; ¼lb. 75c; 1 to 4 lbs., $2.00 per lb.; 5 to 24 lbs., $1.85 per lb.

516 Chicago Warted Hubbard. 115 days. The largest and most popular of the green Hubbards. Pkt. 10c; oz. 25c; ¼lb. 75c; 1 to 4 lbs., $2.00 per lb.; 5 to 24 lbs., $1.85 per lb.

519 Butternut. 85 days. An exceptionally meaty variety of excellent quality. The golden buff fruits are bottle shaped, 10 to 12 inches long and 4 to 5 inches in diameter at the large end. The thick neck is solid; orange-colored flesh, dry, sweet, fine textured and of excellent flavor. Very productive and a good keeper. Pkt. 10c; oz. 30c; ¼lb. $1.10; 1 to 4 lbs., $3.25 per lb.

524 Mammoth Table Queen. 85 days. Has all the qualities of the regular Table Queen but the fruits are larger—6 to 7 inches in diameter. The flesh is light orange, with dry sweet flavor and up to 1½ inches thick. Pkt. 10c; oz. 20c; ¼lb. 55c; 1 to 4 lbs., $1.50 per lb.; 5 to 24 lbs., $1.35 per lb.

525 Uconn. New bush type Acorn Squash. A trial planting will demonstrate its advantages. See page 4.

Summer Varieties

¼ pound will plant about 100 hills, 5 to 6 pounds an acre

503 Caserta. An All-America Selection. This new summer Squash outclasses and outyields older varieties of its type. The fruits are produced near the center of the plant, where they are more easily picked. When 5 to 7 inches long they have a rich buttery flavor far superior to that of any other summer Squash. Pkt. 10c; oz. 25c; ¼lb. 65c; 1 to 4 lbs., $2.00 per lb.

506 Early White Bush. 55 days. Fruits are rather small and quite flat, with scalloped edges. They are produced in amazing quantities, and if kept picked will bear until frost. Snow-white at all times.

510 Early Yellow Summer Crookneck. 50 days. Fruits heavily warted, golden yellow in color.

512 Zucchini Black. 55 days. Fruits long and slender, showing a black-green color when young.

All Summer Squash, except Caserta, pkt. 10c; oz. 20c; ¼lb. 55c; 1 to 4 lbs., $1.50 per lb.; 5 to 24 lbs., $1.35 per lb.

SWISS CHARD

¼ pound will plant 250 feet of row, 10 pounds an acre

496 Fordhook Giant. The rich dark green leaves are very crinkled, thick, and quite tender, making excellent boiling greens. Pkt. 10c; oz. 15c; ¼lb. 40c; 1 to 4 lbs., 95c per lb.; 5 to 24 lbs., 85c per lb.

498 Rhubarb Chard. A valuable novelty, with dark green crumpled leaves above bright crimson stalks. Very attractive in appearance and excellent in flavor. Pkt. 10c; oz. 25c; ¼lb. 70c; 1 to 4 lbs., $2.00 per lb.

TOMATOES
536 Earliana Special   530 P.-W.'s Early Canner

CULTURAL NOTE

P.-W.'s Early Canner and Pritchard (determinate vine types) may be grown successfully on heavily manured or fertilized soil.

Other varieties (larger vine types) produce best on light sandy loam or soil of only average fertility. Excessive fertilization of this type will produce over-abundant vine growth, with greatly reduced yield.

TOMATOES

The Pride of Your Garden and Table

An ounce will produce about 2,000 plants. Approximate number of days from setting plants to ripened fruits is indicated

530 **P.-W.'s Early Canner.** 70 days. The fruits are smooth, very red, and not susceptible to cracks. Vines are compact in habit, allowing three in the space ordinarily required for two. Many years have been spent in tests and selection, to combine the virtues that make it an outstanding variety for all gardeners. Pkt. 10c; ½oz. 60c; oz. 95c; ¼lb. $3.25; lb. $9.50.

536 **Earliana Special.** 66 days. Our strain is the finest of this first-early type. Fruits are medium size, flattened globe shape, deep scarlet-red, firm and smooth. Pkt. 10c; ½oz. 50c; oz. 80c; ¼lb. $2.50; lb. $7.00.

544 **Rutgers.** 80 days. This large, round, firm-fruited Tomato is gaining in popularity. It is valued for canning, where it holds up well in solid pack, and for making sparkling bright red juice of the most excellent flavor. The heavy interior walls ripen from the inside out, making it very desirable also for slicing. Pkt. 10c; ½oz. 35c; oz. 60c; ¼lb. $1.75; 1 to 4 lbs., $5.50 per lb.

540 **Stokesdale.** 70 days. An excellent medium-early Tomato, ripening in the season of John Baer and adapted for market and canning. The fruit is medium size, deep globe shape, very solid and of fine quality. Very productive. Pkt. 10c; ½oz. 35c; oz. 60c; ¼lb. $2.00; lb. $6.00.

542 **Stone** (Improved). 86 days. Enormous yielder. Valuable for the home gardener or canner. Bright deep scarlet fruits, large and flat but deep, smooth and solid. Pkt. 10c; ½oz. 30c; oz. 50c; ¼lb. $1.50; lb. $4.50.

Miniature Tomatoes

556 **Huckleberry** (Wonderberry)
550 **Yellow Pear**
546 **Red Cherry**
554 **Ground Cherry**
Each of above, pkt. 10c; ½oz. 65c; oz. $1.00

RUTABAGA

578 **Laurentian.** 110 days. A preferred strain of the American Purple-Top variety that is practically neckless and has fewer side roots. The flesh is creamy yellow, firm, mild and sweet. Pkt. 10c; oz. 15c; ¼lb. 40c; 1 to 4 lbs., $1.25 per lb.

12

TURNIPS

An ounce will plant 300 feet of row, 1 to 1½ pounds an acre in drills

560 **Purple-Top White Globe** (Special Strain). Large, smooth and of delicious flavor. The color is snow-white, with a rich purple top; the flesh is firm, fine grained and tender. It has become the standard home, truck-garden and shipping variety. Pkt. 10c; oz. 15c; ¼lb. 40c; 1 to 4 lbs., $1.10 per lb.; 5 to 24 lbs., $1.00 per lb.

WATERMELON

A packet will plant about 8 hills, an ounce 25 to 30 hills, 2 to 3 pounds an acre

322 **Kleckley Sweet No. 6** (Wilt Resistant). 88 days. A selected type that has proved almost fully resistant to wilt. Slightly smaller than Improved Kleckley Sweet but otherwise identical. Pkt. 10c; oz. 20c; ¼lb. 55c; 1 to 4 lbs., $1.65 per lb.

326 **Green Klondike** (Wilt Resistant). 90 days. Solid dark green, showing light ribs running lengthwise. Truly delicious. Pkt. 10c; oz. 25c; ¼lb. 70c; 1 to 4 lbs., $2.00 per lb.; 5 to 24 lbs., $1.90 per lb.

328 **Striped Klondike** (Blue Ribbon). 90 days. A new selection of the attractive and universally popular shipping melon, which carries the highest sugar content of any commercial variety. The rind is thin but strong; the flesh is solid and bright red. Average weight is 30 pounds. Pkt. 10c; oz. 25c; ¼lb. 70c; 1 to 4 lbs., $2.00 per lb.; 5 to 24 lbs., $1.90 per lb.

332 **King and Queen** (Winter). 85 days. An excellent shipper. Flesh is sweet and crisp. When properly stored, remains edible for several months. The color is light cream with faint, irregular green stripes. Seeds are quite small and black. Pkt. 10c; oz. 25c; ¼lb. 70c; 1 to 4 lbs., $1.75 per lb.; 5 to 24 lbs., $1.65 per lb.

VEGETABLE ROOTS

ASPARAGUS ROOTS, 2-yr.-old

75 roots will plant 100 feet of row

Cat. No.	10 to 24 roots each	25 to 99 roots each	100 to 249 roots each	250 to 1000 roots each
7000 Mary Washington	$0 07	$0 05	$0 04	$0 03
7002 New Paradise	08	06	05	04

Shipping weight, 2 lbs. per 10; 10 lbs. per 100; 75 lbs. per 1000
For Asparagus seed, see page 5.

HORSE-RADISH

Roots should be set 15 to 20 inches apart, small end down and covered with 2 inches of soil in rows.

7006 **Maliner Kren.** This is considered superior to common Horse-Radish. 10 to 24, 9c each; 25 to 99, 6c each; 100 to 249, 4c each; 250 to 1000, 3c each.

RHUBARB OR PIE-PLANT

7007 **Victoria.** 25c each; 3 to 9, 17c each; 10 to 29, 12c each; 30 to 100, 10c each.

7009 **MacDonald Red.** Now generally considered the best red Rhubarb obtainable. The stalks are very large and bright crimson in color. They are tender, of excellent flavor and when cooked they make a delicious deep pink sauce. Propagated only from divisions. Strong roots, 65c each; 3 to 9, 60c each; 10 to 29, 55c each; 30 to 100, 50c each. Shipping weight, 1½ lbs. each.

SAGE (Salvia officinalis)

6070 One-yr. plants, 50c each; 3 to 9, 45c each; 10 to 29, 40c each. Shipping weight, ½ lb. each.

916 **ALYSSUM, Violet Queen. Pkt. 10c**

PORTER • WALTON'S

Finest

ANNUA
SEEDS

For Quick Growth—
Early and Continuous
Blooming

The amazing modern flowers such as Royal Velvet Cockscomb, Tetra Snapdragons and Fire Chief Petunias (see page 15) radiate a degree of beauty far beyond that of ordinary varieties of a few years past.

1048 **COCKSCOMB, Tall Royal Velvet. Pkt. 20c**

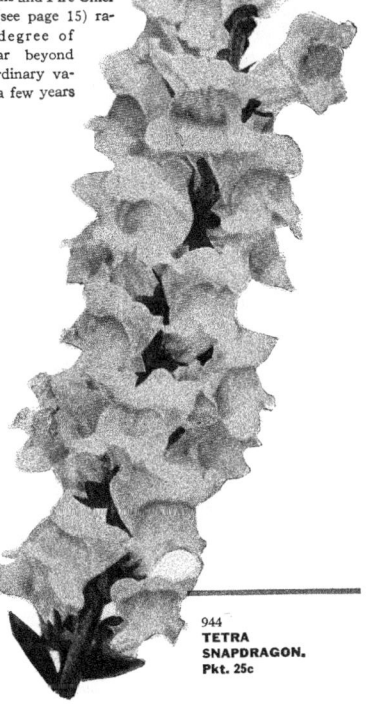

944
**TETRA
SNAPDRAGON.
Pkt. 25c**

1124 **COSMOS, Sensation Mixed. Pkt. 10¢**

1384 PANSIES · Roggli's Swiss Giants
Truly giant blooms 4 to 5 inches across. Wonderful form and color range.
Pkt. 50c; ¼₂oz. $1.75.

1127 UNWIN DAHLIAS · Dwarf Hybrids
2 ft. Early-flowering, semi-double Dahlias on bushy plants. Varied colors. Plant the seeds early. Pkt. 20c.

1275 MARIGOLD . Midget Harmony
8 in. Compact, ball-shaped plants fine for potting or for edging in the garden. Golden yellow bordered maroon-red. Pkt. 10c; ⅛oz. 35c.

1278 MARIGOLD · Single French, Red Head
12 in. A crested center of gold and maroon surrounded by broad overlapping petals of rich mahogany-red. Vigorous, bushy plants. Pkt. 15c; ¼₆oz. 40c.

1446

NEW

POR

1439 **PETUNIA** · **Alderman**

12 to 18 inches. Fairly uniform growth and dark violet blue flowers of velvety appearance. Pkt. 25c; ½oz. 45c.

1446

NEW PETUNIA, FIRE CHIEF

GOLD MEDAL WINNER

All-America Winner for 1950

The reddest Petunia grown. The plants are dwarf and com-pact, very free blooming. The vivid coloring of this new Petunia will amaze you. Pkt. 50c.

PHLOX Drummondi

PHLOX DRUMMONDI

1462 **All Colors Mixed.** 15 in. The bushy, half-spreading plants are excellent for bedding and low, informal borders. They bear large heads of clear, bright-colored flowers. Pkt. 10c; ⅛oz. 40c.

PORTULACA

1480 **P.-W.'s Large-flowering Single Mixed.** 4 in. Pkt. 10c; ⅛oz. 25c.

1490 **P.-W.'s Double Mixture.** 4 in. Pkt. 10c; ⅛oz. 35c.

1480 **PORTULACA, Single Mixed.**

1332 **NASTURTIUMS GLEAM HYBRIDS**

GLEAM HYBRID NASTURTIUMS

Sweet fragrance and long-stemmed double flowers have won many admirers for this excellent garden annual. Their profusion of blooms in lovely cheerful colors makes a beautiful border.

1324 **Golden Gleam.** 12 in. A blaze of golden yellow.
1328 **Scarlet Gleam.** 12 in. Fiery orange-scarlet.
1332 **Gleam Hybrids.** 12 in. A gorgeous color array.

Each of above,
Pkt. 10c; oz. 35c; ¼ lb. $1.00; lb. $3.00

SWEET PEAS
Early-Flowering Spencer. 6 ft.

This new type is in great demand for forcing under glass and for outdoor culture, coming into flower five or six weeks earlier than the summer-flowering type. If flowers are kept picked, will continue to bloom over a period of nearly four months.

1552 **Bridesmaid.** Deep silvery pink; long stems.
1553 **Bright Light.** Flaming scarlet.
1556 **Fragrance.** Large clear lavender, ruffled and fragrant.
1558 **Hope Improved.** Mammoth pure white.
1561 **Princess Blue.** Large light blue.
1566 **Sterling.** Large salmon-rose on strong stems.
1567 **Tops.** Delicate rose-pink. Extra large and wavy.
1570 **Treasure Island.** Golden orange; very large.
1572 **P.-W.'s Early-flowering Spencer, Best Mixed.** The above and many other varieties properly blended for a harmonious color effect.

Each of above, Pkt. 15c; ½ oz. 45c; oz. 80c;
¼ lb. $2.50; lb. $7.50

1572 **SWEET PEAS**
Early-Flowering Spencer

16

PORTER-WALTON COMPANY

P.-W.'S FINEST ANNUAL SEEDS

AGERATUM

904 **Midget Blue.** 3 to 4 in. The low, mound-like plants make exceptionally pretty, narrow ribbon borders of lavender-blue. Pkt. 35c.

ALYSSUM

914 **Snow Cloth (Procumbens).** 4 in. The dwarfest, most compact variety in the Alyssum family. Its moderately spreading habit is highly valued for borders. Pkt. 10c; ⅛oz. 30c.

916 **Violet Queen.** 5 in. Dwarf, neatly compact, and free flowering. Violet shades. Pkt. 10c; ⅛oz. 35c.

Antirrhinum Nanam Grandiflorum SEMI-DWARF SNAPDRAGONS

16 to 20 in. The plants of the Nanum strain are neat, compact and upright and produce simultaneously ten to sixteen well-proportioned flower-spikes. Because of their medium low, sturdy habit and the fact that they require no staking, they are recommended exclusively for garden beds and borders. Cutting the blooms encourages growth of new spikes, keeping the beds in flower all season.

927 **Dainty.** Soft pink flowers.

929 **Harmony.** Combinations of terra-cotta and yellow with shades of rose.

931 **Red Rocket.** Bright gleaming red on strong, base-branched stems.

933 **Rose Sensation.** Rich rose-pink.

947 **Super Majestic Mixture.** Hundreds of shades and color combinations.

New Tall Snapdragon

944 **Tetra Snapdragons.** The exceptionally large flowers are prettily ruffled, produced in larger spikes on 30-inch stems. Base branching in habit, the giant spikes are all long stemmed. Wonderful for cutting.

Each of above, pkt. 25c

BALSAM · Lady-Slipper

1006 **Double Camellia-flowered Mixture.** 18 in. An improved variety that blooms continuously. Many colors. Pkt. 10c; ⅛oz. 35c.

ASTERS

The Aster, with its various colors and fine branching habit, is one of the most satisfactory annual flowering plants.

955 **PRINCESS ASTERS MIXED.** 20 in. A very charming, wilt-resistant strain. The Princess Asters have a full crested center surrounded by rows of broader guard petals, giving a slightly more formal effect. They bloom early and have splendid keeping qualities. Pkt. 15c; 1/32 oz. 35c.

EARLY AMERICAN BEAUTY. 2 to 2½ ft. Wilt resistant.

960 **White**	966 **Crimson**	970 **Deep Rose**
962 **Light Blue**	968 **Shell-Pink**	972 **Mixed**
964 **Dark Blue**		

Each of above, pkt. 10c; 1/16 oz. 30c

GIANT CREGO. 2 to 2½ ft. Wilt resistant. Large flowers with curled petals on 12-inch stems.

974 **White**	978 **Crimson**	982 **Light Blue**
976 **Rose-Pink**	980 **Dark Blue**	984 **Mixed**

Each of above, pkt. 10c; ⅛oz. 35c

994 **El Monte (Super Giant).** 2 ft. Brilliant, glowing crimson. Pkt. 15c; 1/32oz. 35c.

996 **Los Angeles (Super Giant).** 2 ft. Pure shell-pink. Pkt. 15c; 1/32oz. 35c.

Celosia · COCKSCOMB

1046 **Crested Dwarf Mixed.** 15 in. Fine dwarf habit with broad, compact plumes resembling giant rooster combs. Pkt. 10c; 1/16oz. 25c.

1050 **Plumosa Magnifica Mixed.** 2½ to 3 ft. Pastel shades. Pkt. 10c; ⅛oz. 35c.

1048 **Tall Royal Velvet.** 24 in. The tall center stem and its many long branches produce heads or combs of rich crimson. (See page 13.) Pkt. 20c.

IMPROVED GIANT DOUBLE CALENDULAS

The easiest of all annual flowers to grow and also one of the most useful for garden beds or for cutting. They begin blooming when quite young, and if kept picked will flower until frost.

1012 **Chrysantha or Sunshine.** 18 in. Large flowers with overlapping petals of rich buttercup-yellow. Pkt. 10c; ¼oz. 35c.

1016 **Orange King.** Glowing orange with incurved center petals. Pkt. 10c; ¼oz. 25c.

1018 **Double Giant Mixed.** All colors. Pkt. 10c; ¼oz. 20c.

Centaurea · BACHELORS-BUTTON

1056 **Cyanus, Jubilee Gem.** 12 in. Large, fully double flowers of intensified blue. Pkt. 10c; ⅛oz. 25c.

1058 **Cyanus Mixed.** 2 ft. A double-flowering mixture of many colors. Pkt. 10c; ⅛oz. 20c.

1060 **Sweet Sultan (Imperialis Mixed).** 2½ ft. Large, long-stemmed, sweet-scented flowers with finely fringed petals. Pkt. 10c; ⅛oz. 35c.

Cheiranthus · SIBERIAN WALLFLOWER

1070 **Golden Bedder.** 12 in. A very free-flowering plant producing golden yellow flowers. Pkt. 10c; ⅛oz. 20c.

CLARKIA

1080 **Elegans Double Mixed.** 15 in. The flowers are best described as resembling sprays of double-flowering almond. Pkt. 10c; ⅛oz. 20c.

COSMOS

GIANT EARLY-FLOWERING SENSATION. 5 to 6 ft. Unusually large flowers, 3 to 4 inches in diameter, and new colors make Sensation the favorite strain.

1114 **Dazzler.** Rich, deep crimson. Pkt. 10c; ⅛oz. 25c.

1118 **Pinkie.** Sparkling rose-pink. Pkt. 10c; ⅛oz. 25c.

1120 **Purity.** Pure, glistening white. Pkt. 10c; ⅛oz. 25c.

1122 **Radiance.** Large flowers on long stems; deep rose with rich crimson center. Under artificial light they become even more glowing and velvety in appearance. Radiance is 1948 winner of the Silver Medal in the All-America Selections Trials. Pkt. 15c; 1/16oz. 40c.

1124 **Mixed Colors.** Many beautiful shades. Pkt. 10c; ⅛oz. 25c.

1106 **Early Double.** 5 ft. Medium-sized flowers with double crested centers. Pkt. 10c; 1/16oz. 40c.

Cynoglossum · CHINESE FORGET-ME-NOT

1130 **Firmament.** 18 in. A dwarf type of Chinese Forget-Me-Not with flowers of vivid indigo-blue. Bronze Medal Winner. Pkt. 10c; ¼oz. 30c.

DAHLIA HYBRIDS

1127 **Unwin Dwarf.** Many colors. Single flowers in forms of artistic simplicity. Sow seed in early spring. (See page 14.) Pkt. 20c.

Dianthus · CARNATION

1040 **Giant Marguerite Mixed.** 15 in. Begins to flower a few weeks after sowing seed. Pkt. 10c.

Dianthus · GARDEN PINKS

1132 **Single Brilliant Mixed.** 10 in. Pkt. 10c; ⅛oz. 25c.

1134 **Double Heddewigi Mixed.** 10 in. Pkt. 10c; ⅛oz. 20c.

ANNUALS, Continued on Page 18

P.-W.'S FINEST ANNUAL SEEDS

Eschscholtzia · CALIFORNIA POPPY

1023 **Orange King** (Aurantiaca). 8-in. Graceful spreading plants with bright orange flowers. Pkt. 10c; ¼oz. 20c.

GODETIA

Gardeners in higher valleys where the summers are comparatively cool find these showy flowers unexcelled.

1158 **Dwarf Single Mixed.** 12 in. Pkt. 10c; ⅛oz. 35c.

GOURDS

Large Gourd fruits make attractive decorations at harvest festivals, and the smaller ones may be arranged in bowls for the table. Bird houses, dippers, bowls, and toys are made of others.

1164 **All Varieties Mixed.** 8 ft. Pkt. 10c; ½oz. 20c.

Gypsophila · BABY'S-BREATH

1168 **Elegans, Covent Garden.** 2 ft. Large, pure white. Blooms three months from sowing. Pkt. 10c; ½oz. 20c.

Helianthus · SUNFLOWER

1175 **Sungold.** 4½ ft. Fully double, chrysanthemum-like flowers of rich golden orange. Blooms 4 inches across are produced in 70 days from sowing. Pkt. 10c; ¼oz. 25c.

Helichrysum · STRAWFLOWER

1170 **ALL COLORS MIXED.** 2 ft. Pkt. 10c; ⅛oz. 45c.

Iberis · CANDYTUFT

1036 **GIANT HYACINTH-FLOWERED WHITE.** 12 in. Large spikes of snowy white flowers. Pkt. 10c; ¼oz. 30c.

1038 **UMBELLATA, FINEST MIXED.** 12 in. Spreading habit. Pkt. 10c; ¼oz. 25c.

Ipomoea · MORNING-GLORY

1291 **Crimson Rambler.** The best red Morning-Glory for planting with Heavenly Blue and Pearly Gates. The color is ruby-red with white throat. Pkt. 10c; ¼oz. 20c.

1298 **Heavenly Blue.** Clear sky-blue shading to creamy white in the throat. It blooms very early and continues until frost. Pkt. 10c; ¼oz. 30c.

1294 **Pearly Gates.** Early flowering; pure white. Like Heavenly Blue in its nature of growth, size and quantity of bloom. Pkt. 10c; ⅛oz. 35c.

1300 **Mixed.** All colors. Pkt. 10c; ½oz. 20c.

LARKSPUR

The new King strains are the finest of all Larkspurs. In size, in richness and clarity of color, and in abundance of flowers they have not been equaled. Together with the Giant Imperial strain they complete a fine color assortment.

1202 **Blue Spire.** Blue.
1204 **Lilac King.** Lilac.
1206 **Los Angeles.** Salmon.
1208 **Rose King.** Rose.
1210 **White King.** White.
1218 **Giant Imperial Mixed.** These and other beautiful shades.

Each of above, pkt. 10c; ⅛oz. 35c; ¼oz. 55c

LOBELIA

1224 **Crystal Palace Compacta.** 6 in. Rich, deep blue. Dark foliage. Pkt. 10c; 1/32oz. 45c.

Mirabilis · FOUR O'CLOCKS

1148 **Mixed Colors.** 2 ft. Showy plants that do well everywhere. Flowers open in the afternoon except on cloudy days, when they bloom all day. Pkt. 10c; ¼oz. 20c.

MARIGOLD

1256 **All-Double Orange.** 4 ft. Large orange flowers of the improved African type. Pkt. 10c; ⅛oz. 45c.

1260 **All-Double Lemon.** 4 ft. A clear lemon-yellow of large size. Pkt. 10c; ⅛oz. 45c.

1264 **All-Double Mixture.** 4 ft. Extra-large, double flowers in particularly well-blended colors. Pkt. 10c; ⅛oz. 45c.

1266 **Gypsy Jewels.** 18 in. A dwarf-growing form of the popular Gigantea type, producing flowers 4 to 4½ inches in diameter in shades of orange, yellow and primrose. Pkt. 10c; ⅛oz. 25c.

1262 **Mammoth Mum.** 2½ ft. The largest of the "Mum"-flowered Marigolds. The long, sturdy stems hold fluffy, ball-like blooms of pleasing sulphur-yellow. Pkt. 15c; 1/16oz. 60c.

1280 **Sunkist.** 7 in. Silver Medal Winner. Glowing golden yellow. Grand for bedding, borders or pot culture. Pkt. 10c; ⅛oz. 35c.

1284 **Signata Pumila (Gnome).** 6 in. Delicate, fern-like leaves and single flowers of bright golden yellow. Pkt. 10c; 1/16oz. 25c.

SINGLE NASTURTIUMS

1310 **Best Tall Single Mixed.** 2 ft. Pkt. 10c; oz. 35c.

1314 **Best Dwarf Single Mixed.** 12 in. Pkt. 10c; oz. 35c; ¼lb. $1.00; lb. $3.00.

NICOTIANA

The flowers open toward evening and emit a pleasing perfume.

1370 **Affinis Choice Mixed.** 2 ft. Pkt. 10c; ¼oz. 35c.

PANSIES

1380 **Giant International Mixture.** Includes the richest reds, coppers and bronzes, together with the most delicate rose-pink shades. Pkt. 50c; 1/32oz. $1.35.

1384 **Roggli's Swiss Giants.** Well-rounded flowers, 4 to 5 inches across, in excellent mixture. Pkt. 50c; 1/32oz. $1.75.

1392 **Rocky Mountain Giants.** An outstanding Mountain-grown strain of Swiss origin. Large flowers and wonderful colors. Pkt. 50c; 1/16oz. $1.75.

Swiss Giants in Color

1402 **Alpenglow.** Rich garnet-red.
1398 **Berna.** Dark violet-blue.
1400 **Coronation Gold.** The best true golden yellow.
1408 **Lake of Thun.** Marine-blue.
1404 **Rhinegold.** Large yellow with dark center.
1406 **Swiss White.**

Each of above, pkt. 50c; 1/16oz. $2.00

1420 **Scotch or Tufted Pansies** (*Viola cornuta*). 5 in. Dainty flowers in many fine colors; useful for rock gardens, edging beds and borders. Requires protection during winter. Pkt. 50c; 1/32oz. $1.00.

Papaver · POPPY

1470 **American Legion.** Single, orange-scarlet with maltese cross.

1472 **Shirley, All-Double Mixture.** Full range of colors.

1474 **Shirley, Single Mixed.** Crepe-like flowers of various colors.

Each of above, pkt. 10c; ¼oz. 30c; oz. 80c.

1262 MARIGOLD, Mammoth Mum

PETUNIAS
Giant-Flowering Fringed

1422 **Dwarf Giants of California (Ramona Strain).** Dwarf; ruffled and fringed, with open, well-marked throats. Pkt. 50c.

Giant-Flowering Single

1430 **Elk's Pride (Improved Purple Prince).** Largest, darkest and best velvety purple. Pkt. 50c; 1/64oz. $2.50.

1429 **Snowstorm Improved.** The most beautiful of all white Petunias. A shadow of yellow in the throat adds extra richness to the glistening white of the 4 to 5-inch blooms. Pkt. 50c.

Nana Compacta

For continuous profusion of bloom, vivid coloring and ease of culture, this class of Petunia is unsurpassed. Of more dwarf habit, very neat and compact.

1432 **Celestial Rose.** 12 to 15 in. A beautiful rich satiny rose. Pkt. 25c; 1/32oz. 45c.

1433 **Glow.** 10 to 23 in. All-America Silver Medal Winner. One of the finest red dwarf Petunias; 2½-inch flowers of dazzling carmine-red. Pkt. 25c; 1/32oz. 60c.

1443 **Snow Mountain.** 12 to 15 in. Compact. Pure satiny white. Pkt. 25c; 1/32oz. 60c.

1444 **Topaz Queen.** 12 to 15 in. Scarlet-rose of unusual depth, which does not fade. Its flowers are larger than the average of this type. Pkt. 25c; 1/32oz. 60c.

1445 **Nana Compacta Mixture.** 12 in. A wonderful color mixture in the dwarf class. Makes neater beds or borders. Pkt. 20c; 1/32oz. 45c.

Ruffled Nana Compacta

1423 **Little Giants.** 12 in. Ball-shaped plants with medium-sized, ruffled flowers. Their neat habit will please you. Pkt. 50c.

All-Double

1447 **Mixed.** This new strain has fully double, daintily fringed flowers, 2½ to 3 inches in diameter. The colors include many lovely shades and combinations of rose, pink, purple, white and cream. 125 seeds $2.00; 500 seeds $5.00.

Ricinus · CASTOR BEAN

1500 **Zanzibarensis Mixed.** 10 in. The giant leaves are 1 to 2 feet across. Pkt. 10c; oz. 35c.

SALPIGLOSSIS

1504 **Emperor Mixed.** 2½ ft. Large improved strain. Complete range of colors, each with gold veining. Pkt. 10c; 1/8oz. 30c.

SALVIA

1520 **America (Globe of Fire).** 18 in. Uniform in habit of growth and flowering; bright scarlet. Pkt. 50c.

1521 **Blaze of Fire.** 14 to 16 in. Extra early. The plants are strong and floriferous; brilliant red flower spikes. Pkt. 50c.

SCABIOSA

1540 **P.-W.'s Giant Hybrids.** Includes all the new and rare colors. An unrivaled mixture. Pkt. 10c; 1/8oz. 25c.

SCARLET RUNNER BEAN

1542 Bright scarlet, pea-shaped blossoms, followed by delicious edible beans, on plants 8 feet tall. Oz. 10c; 1/4lb. 30c.

STOCKS

1620 **Improved Ten Weeks Mixed.** 12 in. Dwarf, compact, branching plants excellent for bedding. Fragrant flowers of many colors. Pkt. 10c; 1/8oz. 35c.

GIANT SWEET PEAS
Summer-Flowering Spencer. 6 ft.

We offer the very choicest and most distinctive varieties. Each one in its respective color is sure to give entire satisfaction.

1580 **Bonnie Briar.** Immense rose-pink.

1582 **Capri.** Light blue; long stems.

1588 **Flora.** Clear deep lavender.

1590 **Golden Dragon.** Large bright orange, blended orange-rose.

1598 **Rubicund.** Crimson-scarlet.

1600 **Snow-White.** Large solid paper-white.

1604 **Welcome.** Dazzling scarlet on excellent stems.

1610 **P.-W.'s Silver Medal Blend.** The finest assortment of Giant Spencers obtainable at any price. A formula mixture containing 75 named varieties, including the latest novelties.

Each of above, Pkt. 10c; 1/2oz. 25c; oz. 45c; 1/4lb. $1.25; lb. $3.50

1613 **CUTHBERTSON SWEET PEAS.** A new midseason Sweet Pea. It has remarkable heat resistance, vigorous growth and long stems. The flowers are plainer than Spencers, but large and of excellent color. It is preferable to Summer-flowering Spencers where the summers are hot and early. **Finest Mixed.** Pkt. 10c; 1/2oz. 25c; oz. 45c; 1/4lb. $1.25; lb. $3.50.

VERBENA

1652 **Giant Hybrids Mixed.** 12 in. A selected free-blooming strain with large flowers and a wonderful blend of colors. Pkt. 10c; 1/16oz. 40c.

ZINNIA
Giant Dahlia-Flowered

The abundant flowers aften measure 4 inches in depth and 4 to 6 inches across. They are the most desirable of all the large double Zinnias.

1680 **Canary Bird.** Primrose-yellow.

1682 **Crimson Monarch.** Flaming crimson.

1684 **Dream.** Deep lavender-blue.

1686 **Exquisite.** Light rose with deep rose center.

1690 **Polar Bear.** White.

1696 **Giant Dahlia-Flowered, Gold Medal Mixed.**

Each of above, Pkt. 10c; 1/8oz. 35c; 1/4oz. 55c; oz. $1.65

Lilliput 18 in.

1712 **Choice Mixture.** Symmetrical plants with numerous miniature double flowers. The colors range from lilac through red, salmon and yellow to white. Very desirable for cut-flower arrangements. Pkt. 10c; 1/8oz. 25c; 1/4oz. 45c; oz. $1.35.

FERTILIZERS

VIGORO
COMPLETE PLANT FOOD

IMPROVED
FORMULA
6-10-4

"Best for Intermountain
Soils"

Regular feeding—4 pounds
• per 100 square feet.

4008 VIGORO

5 lbs.	$0 50
10 lbs.	90
25 lbs.	1 75
50 lbs.	3 00
100 lbs.	5 00

5 bags or more, $4.50
· per cwt.

f.o.b. Salt Lake City

4001 AMMONIUM SULFATE

A quick-acting, easily soluble fertilizer containing 20%
nitrogen. It stimulates top growth and manufactures plant
cells. It is a valuable plant food for leafy vegetables,
lawns, shrubs and trees. 10 lbs. 65c; 25 lbs. $1.25; 100 lbs.
$3.50.

4005 BONEMEAL

The plant-nourishing elements (nitrogen and phosphorus)
are liberated slowly, making food available for a long
period. 10 lbs. $1.00; 25 lbs. $2.00; 100 lbs. $7.00.

4006 TREBLE SUPERPHOSPHATE

42% or more available phosphoric acid. For general
garden use apply 10 pounds per 1000 square feet. 10 lbs.
70c; 25 lbs. $1.50.

4123

A proved combination of hormones and vitamins. It
insures the success of your roses. Soak roots of bushes in
Rosetone before planting. Water your established rose
bushes for better growth. ½-oz. pkt. 25c; 3-oz. pkg. $1.00.
FULL DIRECTIONS ON PACKAGE

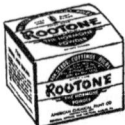
ROOTONE
Reg. U. S. Pat. Off.

4117 Stimulates root growth on
cuttings, bulbs and seeds. Young
plants grow faster, stronger, and
more uniformly. ¼-oz. pkt. 25c;
2-oz. jar $1.00; 1-lb. can $5.00.

IRON SULPHATE

A good corrective for alkaline soils.
4045 **Crystals** for plants, shrubs, trees.
4047 **Snow Form** for lawns.

10 lbs. $1.00; 25 lbs. $2.00; 100 lbs. $7.00

20

4057 SOIL SULPHUR

(99½% pure sulphur.) Sulphur, when disced into the
top soil, changes to sulphuric acid which neutralizes alkali.
The weak sulphuric acid improves fertility by changing
minerals in the soil into a soluble form. It also loosens
heavy soils, improves water penetration, and helps prevent chlorosis. For fertilization apply 2 to 4 pounds per
1000 square feet per year. For improvement or reclamation
of alkaline soils, from 7 to 25 pounds per 1000 square feet
may be needed. 10 lbs. $1.00; 25 lbs. $2.00; 100 lbs. $6.00.

PATENTS PENDING

Reduces Loss in
Transplanting

4119 A hormone-vitamin powder that helps grow new
roots so that plants start growing again in a much
shorter time. Use Transplantone in the garden when
setting out annuals, perennials, shrubs, roses and vegetable or small fruit plants. ½-oz. pkt. 25c; 3-oz. can
$1.00; 1-lb. can $4.00.

4014 PLANTABBS

A complete, balanced
and concentrated plant
food in tablet form for in-
door potted plants and
bulbs.

30 tablets	$0 25
75 tablets	50
200 tablets	1 00
1000 tablets	3 50

PEAT MOSS

4085 One of the most efficient means of adding humus to
the soil. It creates a loamy condition, which aids the
penetration of air and water.

| COMET PEAT MOSS
in convenient sizes | Approximate
Shipping Weight | |
|---|---|---|
| **Large Bale—8 cu. ft.** | 100 lbs. | $4 50 |
| **½ Bale—4 cu. ft.** | 50 lbs. | 3 00 |
| ***Large Bag—2¼ cu. ft.** | 18 lbs. | 1 50 |
| ***Small Bag—¾ cu. ft.** | 6 lbs. | 70 |

*Accepted in mails

Terra-Lite*
BRAND
VERMICULITE
PLANT AID

Perfect as a mulch
for all plants.

GROW BIGGER, BETTER PLANTS

4095 Terra-Lite is a new and better starting medium for
seedlings or cuttings.

Seeds go farther be-
cause germination is
better and there is no
damping off. In the
garden it conditions
and aerates the soil
and conserves mois-
ture.

Great mass of hair
roots in half the time.

Seeds germinate
faster. Virtually no
damping off.

4-qt. bag (1 lb.) $0.39
½-bu. bag (4 lbs.) .85
2-bus. bag (18 lbs.) 1.85

PORTER-WALTON COMPANY

GARDEN AND HOME INSECTICIDES

SPRAYS

3240 VAPOTONE-XX SPRAY

T. E. P. P.—the new wonder insecticide for garden use. Kills aphis, red spider mites, thrips, caterpillars, crawler scale.

4 ozs.	$0 85
16 ozs.	2 50

3440 VOLCK OIL SPRAY

Insecticide, ovicide and spreader for other sprays. Pt. bottle 70c; qt. $1.25; gal. can $2.85.

3400 LEAD ARSENATE

Lb. 60c; 4 lbs. $2.00.

3381 GRASSHOPPER SPRAY

Contains 40% chlorinated camphene. One pound will treat 10,000 square feet. Lb. 75c; 4 lbs. $2.25; 50 lbs. $22.50.

4150 ORTHO LAWN GROOM

Kills weeds and insects and feeds the lawn in one operation. Apply 5 pounds per 1000 square feet. 5 lbs. $1.69; 10 lbs. $2.95.

3316 TRI-OGEN SPRAY. 3-way kit

Tri-ogen is an outstanding all-purpose rose spray and plant stimulant. Mildew and blackspot as well as both chewing and sucking insects are easily controlled with Tri-ogen spray when used as directed.

		Shipping Weight	
E kit protects	6 to 10 roses all summer..	2 lbs.	$1 35
A kit protects	12 to 20 roses all summer..	3 lbs.	2 25
B kit protects	50 to 80 roses all summer..	8 lbs.	6 00
C kit protects	100 to 160 roses all summer..	12 lbs.	9 00

3378 CHLORDANE CONCENTRATE 44%.

An emulsifiable concentrate for the control of grasshoppers ants, roaches, etc. 4-oz. bottle 75c; 8 ozs. $1.25; pt. $2.25.

3290 DDT 50% WETTABLE

Lb. 75c; 4 lbs. $1.75; 50 lbs. $18.00.

3298 ISOTOX GARDEN SPRAY

Containing the new gama isomer from Lindane it kills a greater variety of insects than DDT and has none of the objectionable properties of DDT. Controls aphis, lawn moth earwigs, ants, thrips, flies, wireworms, and many other pests. 2 ozs. 59c; 4 ozs. $1.00; 16 ozs. $2.95; ½gal. $10.25.

3457 RIX SPRAY

This astounding new product is an excellent year-round spray, for dormant or summer spraying. Rix Spray controls mildew, red spider mites, peach-leaf curl, blackspot, scale, rust and other similar pests and diseases. Also used as a corrective for alkaline soils at the rate of 1 quart per 3500 square feet. 4 ozs. 35c; pt. bottle 95c; qt. $1.50; gal. $5.00.

DUSTS

3301 BOTANO DELUXE DUST

A combination of modern chemicals that controls most types of insects as well as fungus and plant diseases. Included are Lindane, which is a penetrating insect killer, and Fermate, the best of the modern fungicides. 8-oz. duster pkg. 85c; 2-lb. bag $1.75; 5-lb. bag $3.95.

3317 ORTHO ROSE DUST

Designed especially to combat the insects and diseases which attack rose plants. May be used also for most chewing and sucking insects and plant diseases in the general flower garden. 8-oz. duster pkg. $1.00; lb. $1.25.

3293 PEST-B-GON DUST

Contains 10% DDT. 10-oz. duster 69c.

3320 ENDOPEST

A multi-purpose dust for the control of many insects, fungi, and plant diseases. 10 ozs. 95c; 2 lbs. $1.90.

3347 SCRAM DOG REPELLENT

A powder in applicator package used to keep dogs away from shrubs, lawns, porches, etc. 8-oz. pkg. 49c.

SEED AND NURSERY SPECIALISTS

BAITS

3387 BUG-GETA PELLETS COMPRESSED BAITS

A Metaldehyde-Arsenical Bait for use against slugs, snails. Easier to use, cleaner to handle, more economical and lasts longer than older-type meal baits. Broadcast baits in evening and clean up dead snails and slugs the next morning.

12 ozs.	$0 35
2 lbs.	75
5 lbs.	1 60

PESTS	CONTROL RECOMMENDED
ANTS	(1) Botano deLuxe
	(2) Chlordane Concentrate 44%
APHIS	(1) Vapotone XX
	(2) Botano deLuxe
BAGWORMS	(1) 50% Wettable DDT.
	(2) Lead Arsenate.
BLACKSPOT	(1) Rix Spray
	(2) Botano deLuxe
BORERS (peach tree)	(1) 50% Wettable DDT in early July
BORERS (soft wood)	(1) Prune and burn infested parts in April
CABBAGE WORM	(1) Volck, plus Lead Arsenate in July
	Vapotone XX before heads form
CODLING MOTH	(1) 50% Wettable DDT plus Vapotone XX
	(2) Lead Arsenate plus Volck
CORN BORER	(1) Pest-B-Gon 10% DDT Dust
CORN EARWORM	(1) Pest-B-Gon 10% DDT Dust
	(2) Ortho Rose Dust
CRABGRASS	(1) Lead Arsenate early spring
	(2) New Weedone early spring
CUTWORM	(1) Bug-geta Pellets
DOGS	(1) Scram Dog Repellent
EARWIGS	(1) Isotox Garden Spray
	(2) Isotox Garden Spray
FLEA BEETLES	(1) Isotox Garden Spray
	(2) Pest-B-Gon 10% DDT Dust
FLIES (house & stable)	(1) Isotox Garden Spray
GRAPE LEAF HOPPER	(1) Botano deLuxe before berries form
	Ortho Rose Dust after berries form
GRASSHOPPERS	(1) Grasshopper Spray
	(2) Chlordane Concentrate 44%
GRUBS (white)	(1) Lead Arsenate
MEALYBUG	(1) Volck plus Vapotone XX
MILDEW (powdery)	(1) Rix Spray (don't use Rix on grapes)
ONION MAGGOT	(1) Botano deLuxe (dust 2 ounces in the topsoil for each 40 square feet)
PEAR SLUG (on pears, cherries, hawthorn, etc.)	(1) Vapotone XX
	(2) Lead Arsenate
PEACH LEAF CURL	(1) Rix Spray (apply in early fall and as a dormant spray in early spring)
PEACH TREE BORER	(1) 50% Wettable DDT in July
PILL BUG	(1) Bug-geta Pellets
POTATO BLIGHT	(1) Ortho Rose Dust
POTATO FLEA BEETLE	(1) Ortho Rose Dust
RED SPIDER MITE	(1) Volck plus Vapotone XX
	(2) Rix Spray
ROACHES	(1) Chlordane Concentrate 44%
	(2) Isotox Garden Spray (Undiluted)
ROSE PESTS (GENERAL)	(1) Tri-ogen (3-way Spray kit)
	(2) Ortho Rose Dust
ROSE SNOUT BEETLE	(1) Botano deLuxe
	(2) Ortho Rose Dust
RUSTS (mite)	(1) Rix Spray
	(2) Botano deLuxe
SCALE	(1) Volck Oil Spray plus Vapotone XX
SHOT HOLE BORER	(1) Fertilize and water to improve health of trees. 50% Wettable DDT in early June and August.
SLUGS & SNAILS	(1) Bug-geta Pellets
SOD WEB WORMS	(1) Ortho Lawn Groom
	(2) Vapotone XX
SOIL INSECTS	(1) Botano deLuxe (For large areas write for recommendation)
SPIDERS	(1) Chlordane Concentrate 44%
SQUASH BUG	(1) Botano deLuxe
STRAWBERRY WEEVILS	(1) Botano deLuxe
TENT CATERPILLARS	(1) Bug-geta Pellets
THRIPS	(2) 50% Wettable DDT
	(1) Botano deLuxe
	(2) Isotox Garden Spray
TOMATO FRUIT WORM	(1) Botano deLuxe
WIREWORM	(1) Botano deLuxe
	(2) Isotox Garden Spray

KILLS WEEDS STERILIZES SOIL

3480 **TRIOX.** Kills annual weeds and top growth of established deep-rooted perennial weeds. Triox sterilizes the soil on walks, drives, patios, tennis courts or any place where no plant growth is wanted. Use 3 pints per 1000 square feet to kill weeds or 3 gallons per 1000 square feet to sterilize the soil. Qt. $1.00; gal. $3.50.

3491 **WEEDONE BRUSH KILLER 32**

A new combination of 2,4-D and 2,4,5-T which kills a wide range of woody plants and prevents sprouting of tree stumps. Valuable for use on farms, ranches, camps, rights-of-way, roadsides and railroads. One to 1½ gallons mixed with 100 gallons of water will treat one acre. Qt. $4.00; gal. $9.25; 5 gals., $8.95 per gal. ($44.75); 54 gals., $8.60 per gal. ($464.40).

The New IMPROVED
3845 **WEEDONE**
TRADE MARK

contains the powerful 2,4,5-T and 2,4-D, the two most effective chemicals for killing lawn weeds, poison ivy, wild plum, wild blackberries, wild morning-glory and over 90 other weeds and woody plants WITHOUT KILLING THE GRASS. Non-poisonous to animals or humans.

Kills a greater variety of lawn weeds and woody plants than any products containing only one of these chemicals. *Does not give off vapors that cause injury to flowers or ornamentals.*

* Prevents re-sprouting of tree stumps.
* The only ALL-PURPOSE weed killer.

CRAB GRASS in lawns can now be prevented with a pre-emergence spray of New Improved WEEDONE. Apply in early spring before the crab grass seed germinates.

8-oz. can.....................$1 00 | 1-gal. can.....................$6 95
1-qt. can.....................2 75 | 5-gal. can.....................25 00

2,4-D CONCENTRATES For Commercial Sprayer
3484 **WEEDAR 64.** The alkanolamine salt form. Gal. $6.00; 5 gals., $5.70 per gal. ($28.50); 54 gals., $5.35 per gal. ($288.90).
3487 **WEEDONE CONCENTRATE 48.** The ethyl ester form. Gal. $7.90; 5 gals., $7.65 per gal. ($38.25); 54 gals., $7.40 per gal. ($399.60).

SPRAYERS AND DUSTERS

4563
CLIMAX SPRAYER with Simplex Inner Seal Top

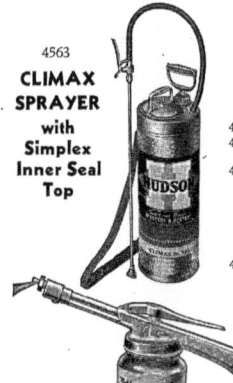

COMPRESSED AIR SPRAYERS
All sprayers are equipped with long-life, oil-resistant hose and gaskets

	Capacity	Shipping Weight	Price
4561 **HUDSON BOOSTER.** Galvanized tank with funnel top	3¼ gals.	9 lbs.	$6 24
4563 **HUDSON CLIMAX.** See illustration. Has new type Simplex Inner Seal Top	3½ gals.	10 lbs.	12 75
4569 **HUDSON PERFECTION.** Galvanized tank with Simplex Inner Seal Top	4 gals.	13½ lbs.	15 65

COMPRESSION BURNER
4598 **HUDSON FLAME SPRAYER.** Produces a 15 to 18-inch flame at 2000 degrees F. Holds 3½ gallons of kerosene and burns about 1 gallon per hour. Shipping weight 22 lbs. $25.00.

4610 **HAYES JR. SPRAY GUN.** Mixes three gallons of spray at a time. Operates on hose with water pressure of 30 to 175 pounds. $6.95 each.

ARMSTRONG SPRAY OUTFIT
Pump made entirely of brass. Nothing to get out of order.
4550 **Pump and Nozzle only.** Weight 4 lbs. $6.25.
4552 **Knapsack only.** Weight 10 lbs. $7.30.
4555 **Armstrong Spray Outfit Complete.** Weight 13½ lbs. $13.50.

POWER SPRAYERS
COMPLETE LINE
On Skids   On Tires
Or Wheelbarrow Model

15 to 150-gallon capacity. Write for 56-page illustrated catalog of sprayers, spray booms, spray nozzles, etc., with new price list.

GARDEN DUSTER
4647 **Hudson Admiral.** Most efficient low-cost Duster for the home garden.

	Chamber	Shipping Weight	Price
	2¾ x 4½ in.	2 lbs.	$1 90

4520 GERMACO HOTKAPS

Individual hothouses protect from frosts, storms and insects. 12 inches in diameter and 6 inches high.

	Shipping Weight	Price
Pkg. of 25 with paper setter	2 lbs.	$0 70
Pkg. of 100 with fibreboard setter	5 lbs.	2 75
Pkg. of 250 with fiberboard setter	10 lbs.	4 65
Carton of 1000	33 lbs.	14 65
5,000 to 9000, per 1000		14 50
10,000 up, per 1000		14 35
4524 Fiberboard Setter	1 lb.	20
4525 Metal Setter	4 lbs.	1 95

4530 GERMACO HOTENTS
Large air capacity. 13 x 16 inches at the base.

Per 500 (1 case), $14.50, 1000 (2 cases), $27.50, f.o.b. Salt Lake City. Shipping weight, 35 lbs. per case.

4533 **Metal Hotent Setter** $2 50

National **Eezy Wear**
Garden Gloves
DURABLE WASHABLE LEATHER

	Per pair
4895 Ladies' Small, Medium	$1 25
4897 Men's Small, Medium	1 35

4888 SWAGGERETTE GLOVES
for house and garden use

Tough, durable natural rubber in attractive green color. Curved fingers and soft lining for extra comfort.

Small	Medium	Large
	All three sizes, 98c per pair	

WOOD POT LABELS

PLAIN

		Per 100	Per 1000
4870	4 in.	$0 40	$3 00
4870	5 in.	40	3 25
4870	6 in.	45	3 75
4870	8 in.	65	5 00

PAINTED

4873	4 in.	45	3 75
4873	5 in.	50	4 00
4873	6 in.	55	4 50
4873	8 in.	80	7 00

TREE LABELS 3½ in., Wired

4860 Plain		$0 45	$3 50
4863 Painted		50	4 25

SEED AND NURSERY SPECIALISTS

MASTERS
"Fertilizer Miser"
Spreaders

Accurate—Finger-Tip Control

	Spread	Capacity	Shipping Weight	Price
4804	18 in.	20 lbs.	13 lbs.	$8 25
4805	18 in.	50 lbs.	19 lbs.	11 50

(Larger spreaders quoted on request)

4819
Saves Seed and Time

SEED SOER 50¢

You will love it - properly distributed seed goes twice as far - saves thinning. For peas to petunias. Cork of 6½" x 1" plastic tube pivots in palm - tap gently. *SATISFACTION GUARANTEED.*

Have flowers and vegetables weeks earlier
with "GRO-QUICK"

ELECTRIC SOIL HEATING CABLE

4915 JUNIOR GRO-QUICK with thermostat and 40-foot 200-watt cable for 3 x 6-foot bed. $6.75 each.

4917 SENIOR GRO-QUICK with thermostat and 80-foot 400-watt cable for 6 x 6-foot bed. $9.00 each.

Instructions included with each unit.

4818 CYCLONE SEED SOWER

A good large sower that meets the most exacting demands. Hangs by strap over shoulders of operator. Hoppersack has 1½ bu. capacity. Broadcasts evenly all varieties of grain and grasses. Shipping weight 4 lbs. $3.75 each.

4857 CEE TEE TREE PROTECTOR

Here is real protection for your young trees. Cee Tee Self-Locking Tree Protectors are made of a semi-rigid plastic material which lasts for years. You can use them many times They guard against rabbits, other rodents, sun scald and winter burn. They prevent trees from splitting as a result of too rapid freezing and thawing. Their fire-resistant properties protect tree bases from damage by grass fires. Furnished in 12-inch units. Two units can be locked together to make a 23-inch protector. 12-inch unit, 49c each. Packed 6 units per carton. Shipping weight, 1 lb. per unit.

Perennial Seeds

1800 **Alyssum saxatile compactum.** BASKET-OF-GOLD.
10 in. Pkt. 10c.

1820 **Aquilegia, Mrs. Scott Elliott's Long-spurred Hybrids.** COLUMBINE. 26 in. Pkt. 10c.

1876 **Campanula medium calycanthema, Mixed Colors.** CUP-AND-SAUCER CANTERBURY BELLS. 2 ft. Pkt. 10c..

1882 **Campanula persicifolia alba.** WHITE PEACHLEAF BELLFLOWER. 2½ ft. Pkt. 25c.

1900 **Coreopsis, Sunburst.** 2 ft. Pkt. 10c.

Pacific Hybrid Delphinium. 6 ft.

1916 **Galahad Series.** White.
1918 **Guinevere Series.** Pinkish lavender with white bee.
1919 **King Arthur Series.** Violet with white bee.
1927 **Percival Series.** White with black bee.
1920 **Summer Skies Series.** Clear light blue.
1914 **Round Table Series.** A mixture of all colors.

· **Each of above, pkt. 50c; ½₂oz. $1.50**

Dianthus barbatus · SWEET WILLIAM
18 in.

2150 **Single Giant-flowered Mixed.** Pkt. 15c.
2160 **Double Giant-flowered Mixed.** Pkt. 15c.
2170 **Newport Pink.** Large, single flowers. Pkt. 15c.
2180 **Scarlet Beauty.** Large, single. Pkt. 15c.

1950 **Digitalis purpurea gloxiniæflora.** FOXGLOVE. 4 ft. Mixed colors. Pkt. 10c.

1994 **Hollyhock, Double Mixed.** 6 ft. Pkt. 10c.

2020 **Lupinus, Russell Strain.** 3 ft. Mixed colors. Pkt. 25c.

2050 **Poppy, Iceland, Sanford's Giants Mixed.** 20 in. Pkt. 25c.

2060 **Primula polyanthus, Giant Munstead Strain.** 8 in. Pkt. 50c.

2070 **Pyrethrum roseum, Single and Double Mixed.** PAINTED DAISY. 2 ft. Pkt. 25c.

6754 GEUM, Mrs. Bradshaw

6629 ARMERIA, Glory of Holland

Perennial Plants

ARMERIA

6629 **Glory of Holland.** 20 in. A new and improved form of Armeria. Tall, straight stems carry 1½-inch, ball-like blooms of clear deep pink throughout the summer. 30c each; 3 to 24, 27c each; 25 to 100, 24c each.

Chrysanthemum maximum
SHASTA DAISY

6699 **Esther Reed.** 18 in. This beautifully formed, fully double Shasta Daisy is much sought after for its lavish garden display and for its exceedingly delightful bouquets. The blooms are 3 inches across and pure white, borne on neat, vigorous plants. 40c each; 3 to 24, 35c each.

GEUM

6754 **Mrs. Bradshaw.** 18 in. Large, double, rich scarlet flowers through the summer. Rich green foliage. 30c each; 3 to 24, 27c each; 25 to 100, 24c each.

BEARDED IRIS

Write for our summer list, which will include Bearded Iris.

SIBERIAN IRIS

6894 **Peggy Perry.** 32 in. Early. Dainty, ruffled flowers of rich violet-blue with a white center. 30c each.
6898 **Snow Queen.** 36 in. An exquisite Iris of snowy whiteness and firm, wax-like texture. 30c each.

LILY-OF-THE-VALLEY

7013 Sold only in bunches of 25 pips. $1.50 per bunch; 3 to 9 bunches, $1.40 each; 10 or more bunches, $1.25 each.

PEONIES

Peonies prefer a well-drained location in full sun. Plant as early as possible in deeply dug soil with bonemeal mixed in the bottom of the hole.
7066 **Unnamed Red**   7068 **Unnamed White**
7067 **Unnamed Pink**
75c each; 3 to 9 of one kind, 65c each

TEUCRIUM

6984 **Chamædrys.** Dense, bushy plants with glossy evergreen foliage resembling dwarf boxwood. Pink flowers in summer. 25c each; 3 to 24, 22c each; 25 to 100, 20c each.

PORTER-WALTON COMPANY

P.-W.'s *Fine* PERENNIALS •

6624 AQUILEGIA
Mrs. Scott Elliott's Long-Spurred Hybrids

Aquilegia · COLUMBINE

6622 Crimson Star. Most striking crimson sepals and spurs with a contrasting white center. An admirable subject in the garden. 35c each; 3 to 24, 32c each; 25 to 100, 28c each.

6624 Mrs. Scott Elliott's Long-Spurred Hybrids. 26 in. Light and airy flowers poised gracefully on slender stems, bloom in a wonderful mixture of both rich and delicate colors. They are very hardy and thrive in sun or part shade. 30c each; 3 to 24, 27c each; 25 to 100, 24c each.

ALYSSUM

6608 Saxatile compactum. Basket-of-Gold. 10 in. The brightest yellow spring rock-garden flower. 30c each; 3 to 24, 27c each; 25 to 100, 24c each.

Campanula
CANTERBURY
BELLS

6708 Medium calycanthema. 2 ft. The old favorite Cup-and-Saucer Canterbury Bell, a flower worthy of perpetuation in every modern garden. 30c each; 3 to 24, 27c each; 25 to 100, 24c each.

6714 White Peachleaf Bellflower. 24 in. Slender, tower-like spikes of pure crystal-white, star-shaped blooms in June and July. Its ease of culture and glistening garden effect will soon make it one of the most popular spire-like white flowers. 30c each; 3 to 24, 27c each; 25 to 100, 24c each.

6712 Cluster Bellflower. 18 in. Compact, upright clusters of small, deep blue bells. 30c each; 3 or more, 27c each.

6717 Harebell (*C. rotundifolia*). 12 in. Thrives in sun or part shade. Has fine foliage and from June to August produces dainty, bright blue flowers. 30c each; 3 to 24, 27c each; 25 to 100, 24c each.

6608 ALYSSUM (Basket-of-Gold)

6708 CAMPANULA Medium calycanthema (Cup-and-Saucer Canterbury Bells)

25

6680 **CHRYSANTHEMUM, Lavender Lady**

GARDEN CHRYSANTHEMUMS

Disbudding to eight to twelve blooms to the plant will produce flowers of exceptional exhibition quality, which will open a week or more earlier than normal. Even without disbudding, however, you will have the best garden Chrysanthemums you have ever grown.

6651 **Burgundy.** 34 in. Glowing wine-red. Strong stems. Sept. 25.

6662 **Gold Standard.** Eng. 36 in. Large double blooms with incurved petals of rich yellow, 7 inches across when disbudded. Oct. 1.

6667 **Hillcrest Red.** Eng. 36 in. Velvety crimson with a golden reverse. Oct. 10.

6669 **Jayeff.** (New.) 24 in. This vigorous, bushy plant bears dozens of straight-stemmed flowers of deep dazzling pink. The blooms are fully double with no center disc, and reach a diameter of 3 to 4 inches. Beginning in mid-September, Jayeff bears continuously until severe frost.

6680 **Lavender Lady.** 30 in. Lovely double flower of true lavender. Unusually clean-cut, beautiful, 3-inch blooms, perfectly spaced on branching sprays. Oct. 5.

6675 **Leda.** Eng. 30 in. Heliotrope-pink, double flowers, 6 to 7 inches across if disbudded. Oct. 5.

6679 **Matador.** Large, globe-shaped blooms made up of many perfectly incurved petals. Attractive lavender-pink. Fully double. Oct. 25.

6673 **Mrs. Pattie.** Eng. 20 in. Terra-cotta-red with gold reverse. A large, deep flower with incurved petals. The very earliest variety. Sept. 15.

6654 **Red Velvet.** 26 in. Best velvety crimson. Oct. 5.

6683 **Rob Roy.** 22 in. Double white. Continuous bloomer from early September until frost.

6658 **White Lady.** Eng. 40 in. Without question, White Lady is one of the finest white Chrysanthemums for the garden. It has shades of primrose in the center that lend a distinct richness to its character. The extra-large flowers are of excellent form. Oct. 10.

Each of above, 40c each; 3 to 24, 35c each; 25 to 100, 32c each. (Shipping weight, 1 lb., 14 ozs., and 12 ozs. per plant respectively.)

6654 **CHRYSANTHEMUM, Red Velvet**

Arabis · ROCK CRESS

6626 **Snow Cap.** 5 in. Dwarf, compact plants with dense masses of shining snow-white flowers. Blooms very early in the spring. 30c each; 3 to 24, 27c each; 25 to 100, 24c each.

26

COREOPSIS

6718 **Sunburst.** 2 ft. Highly prized for cut-flower decorations because of their long, graceful stems and exceptionally long-keeping quality. One of the few perennials that will bloom continuously when the flowers are kept cut. 30c each; 3 to 24, 27c each; 25 to 100, 24c each.

6748 **DIGITALIS, Mixed**

P.-W.'s FINE PERENNIALS

PACIFIC HYBRID DELPHINIUM

Since the introduction of this superb class of giant Delphiniums it has become everyone's favorite. The plants grow 6 feet tall and bear spikes with huge florets 2½ inches and more in diameter that are practically 100 per cent double. Our seed stock comes directly from the originator and our plants are of especially selected strains.

6728 **Galahad Series.** White. 40c each; 3 to 24, 35c each; 25 to 100, 32c each.

6729 **King Arthur.** One of the most brilliant Delphiniums. The color is rich royal purple with a velvety texture and a large white bee. The long spikes are strong and beautifully formed. 40c each; 3 to 24, 35c each; 25 to 100, 32c each.

6726 **Summer Skies Series.** Clear light blue. 40c each; 3 to 24, 35c each; 25 to 100, 32c each.

6724 **Round Table Series.** Many different crosses and blends are included in this mixture. 35c each; 3 to 24, 32c each; 25 to 100, 28c each.

DELPHINIUM, Pacific Hybrids

Digitalis
FOXGLOVE

6748 **Purpurea gloxiniæflora, Mixed.** 4 ft. The long, tubular, spotted flowers hang in a mass on spikes 2 to 3 feet long. The mixture includes purple, rose, yellow and white. 30c each; 3 to 24, 27c each; 25 to 100, 24c each.

Dianthus barbatus
SWEET WILLIAM

6976 18 in. Many rich and sparkling colors in early summer. 30c each; 3 to 24, 27c each; 25 to 100, 24c each.
6980 **Midget Double.** 5 in. Compact, bushy plants with broad clusters of flowers in many bright colors. 30c each; 3 to 24, 27c each; 25 to 100, 24c each.

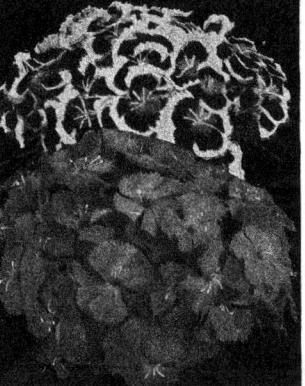

6976 **DIANTHUS BARBATUS** (Sweet William)

DIANTHUS

6740 **Old Spice.** Pat. 499. A choice hybrid of the old-fashioned Garden Pink. Large, carnation-like blooms are rich salmon-pink. Very hardy. 70c each; 3 to 24, 62c each.

6746 **Rose Cushion.** 3 to 4 in. As a border or a dainty novelty, this has no equal. The compact, cushion-like mounds of silver-green foliage are neat and attractive all summer. Dainty, fragrant blooms of brilliant rose color in June. 35c each; 3 to 24, 32c each; 25 to 100, 28c each.

6746 **DIANTHUS, Rose Cushion**

LUPINUS · Lupine

6906 Russell Strain. 3 ft. Long, well-rounded, symmetrical flower spikes of striking beauty. The color range is extensive. 35c each; 3 to 24, 32c each; 25 to 100, 28c each.

PERENNIAL PHLOX

Perennial Phlox is the backbone of the midsummer flower garden. No other perennial offers so many bright glowing colors for this so-called "off season." Deep, loamy, well-fertilized soil, consistent moisture and a little shade in the afternoon are ideal conditions for Phlox.

6922 Africa. Large, well-shaped flower heads. Florets large, brilliant carmine-red with blood-red eye. Strong, mildew-resistant plants.

6929 Fairy King. Large, shapely flower heads with rounded, velvety florets of loveliest lavender marked with a violet eye. It combines beautifully with pink or white varieties. Hardy and unusually disease resistant.

6941 Mary Louise. Large heads of pure waxy white, with individual flowers of enormous size. The best pure white.

6937 Pink Charm. Clear pink with a slight flush of rosy orange. A rich, satisfying color that makes a magnificent clump.

6935 Purple Heart. Individual florets of medium size, carried in good-sized trusses. This eye-catching variety is brilliant deep blue-purple, intensified by a darker center.

Each of above, 40c each; 3 to 24, 35c each; 25 to 100, 32c each

PRIMULA · Primrose

6960 Polyanthus, Giant Munstead Strain. 8 in. A wonderful improved strain of English origin, bearing giant flowers in many new and desirable colors. 35c each; 3 to 24, 32c each; 25 to 100, 28c each.

Pyrethrum · PAINTED DAISY

6968 Roseum. 2 ft. An excellent range of colors. Blooms in May. 35c each; 3 to 24, 32c each; 25 to 100, 28c each.

VINCA

6992 Minor. Grave Myrtle. 4 in. Glossy evergreen foliage forming a dense carpet, sprinkled with blue flowers. 30c each; 3 to 24, 27c each; 25 to 100, 24c each.

6937 **PHLOX, Pink Charm**

6929 **PHLOX, Fairy King**

6906 **RUSSELL LUPINES**

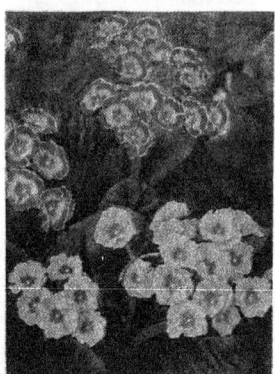

6960 **PRIMULA polyanthus Giant Munstead Strain**

28

PORTER-WALTON COMPANY

ANEMONE

8508 St. Brigid Strain. 8 to 12 in. Lovely flowers of very brilliant colors, excellent for cutting. Many shades of crimson, blue, lavender, heliotrope, rose-pink, white and salmon. 1 to 9, 8c each; 10 to 49, 7c each; 50 up, 6c each.

TUBEROUS-ROOTED BEGONIAS

Few plants can equal the Tuberous-rooted Begonias for brilliancy of color and duration and perfection of bloom in the garden. The ideal situation for them is in filtered sunlight where there is plenty of fresh air, protected from strong winds.

Double Giant Camellia-Flowered
10 to 12 in.

8514 **Pink**	8516 **Salmon**	8518 **Red**
8510 **White**	8512 **Orange**	

Dormant bulbs: 1½ to 2-inch tubers available from February 1 to March 15.

Each of above, 40c each; 3 to 9, 35c each; 10 to 29, 30c each

8597 **ZEPHYRANTHES rosea**

CANNA

8550 City of Portland. 42 in. An appealing shade of rose-pink. Large flowers; broad green foliage.

8552 King Humbert. 48 in. Large scarlet flowers and handsome, broad, bronze foliage.

8554 The President. 42 in. Rich glowing scarlet; immense flowers. Strong stalks and heavy foliage. A free bloomer.

8558 Yellow King Humbert. 48 in. Deep yellow, softly spotted and blotched bright red. Rich green foliage.

Each of above, 20c each; 3 to 9, 18c each; 10 to 29, 16c each

Sprekelia
AZTEC LILY

8579 Flowers similar to amaryllis but much more graceful in form. Dark scarlet. 75c each; 3 to 9, 67c each.

TIGRIDIA
Shellflower

8570 Few flowers are more gorgeously colored. Plant in a sunny position in well-drained soil. They bloom from mid-July to September. 1 to 9, 12c each; 10 to 49, 11c each; 50 up, 10c each.

8579 **SPREKELIA**

TUBEROSE

8586 Mexican Single. Spikes of wax-like, white flowers with rich fragrance. The most graceful variety, best for arrangements. 1 to 9, 12c each; 10 to 49, 11c each; 50 up, 10c each.

Zephyranthes · ZEPHYR LILY

8597 Rosea. 8 to 12 in. Very graceful, star-shaped flowers of rosy pink, blooming all summer. 1 to 9, 15c each; 10 to 49, 14c each; 50 up, 13c each.

8568 **RANUNCULUS Hybrids**

MONTBRETIA

8563 Fire King. 2 to 2½ ft. Very attractive, intense deep red of high garden value.

8566 Giant Mixed. 2 to 2½ ft. The mixture contains many bright shades of yellow, salmon, scarlet and orange. Fine for cutting.

Each of above, 1 to 9, 12c each; 10 to 49, 11c each; 50 up, 10c each

RANUNCULUS

8568 Hybrids. Buttercup. 8 to 12 in. Double flowers up to 3 inches across, in varying shades of red, yellow, orange and pink. 1 to 9, 9c each; 10 to 49, 8c each; 50 up, 7c each.

8513 **TUBEROUS-ROOTED BEGONIA, Orange**

SEED AND NURSERY SPECIALISTS

Continuous Bloom from Summer until Frost

LARGE EXHIBITION CLASS

8658 Blue River. FD. Large; as near to blue as any Dahlia. 60c each; 3 to 9, 54c each.

8641 California Idol. ID. Beautiful clear yellow of immense size. 75c each; 3 to 9, 67c each.

8675 Jersey Dainty. C. Beautiful white, often tinged with pink. 60c each; 3 to 9, 54c each.

8653 Kentucky. FD. Orange tinted pink. A leader for cut-flower or garden use. 60c each; 3 to 9, 54c each.

8629 Queen City. FD. Scarlet-pink, a color without an equal in the flower world. One of the best early cut flowers. 60c each; 3 to 9, 54c each.

8632 San Francisco. D. Large, 12-inch blooms of gorgeous shrimp-pink. One of the best for garden flowers. 60c each; 3 to 9, 54c each.

8622 Scarlet Leader. SC. Geranium-red with shadings of crimson. 60c each; 3 to 9, 54c each.

8665 Town Topic. FD. Ten-inch flowers make a big attraction in deep purple and white. 60c each; 3 to 9, 54c each.

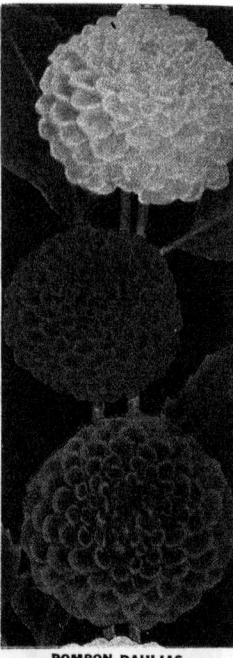

8641
**LARGE
EXHIBITION
DAHLIA
CALIFORNIA IDOL**

**"Big Bouquet"
COLLECTION
No. 8605**

Five Novel Dahlias for cutting or garden display.

One each of:
**SCARLET LEADER
QUEEN CITY
CALIFORNIA IDOL
KENTUCKY
TOWN TOPIC**

5 Beautiful Dahlias

for only **$2.60**

Separately packed and labeled.
Mailing weight 2 lbs.

POMPON DAHLIAS

MINIATURE CLASS

8679 Bishop of Llandaff. Duplex. Rich scarlet flowers and bronze foliage. 60c each; 3 to 9, 54c each.

8686 Coralette. Dec. Lovely coral-pink. 60c each; 3 to 9, 54c each.

8689 Little Roseatta. FD. One of the finest miniatures. Beautiful deep pink. 45c each; 3 to 9, 40c each.

Special Miniature Collection
No. 8607

One each of the three Miniature Dahlias

3 tubers for only **$1.30**

Separately packed and labeled. Mailing weight 1 lb.

POMPON CLASS

These are ball-type Dahlias with compact, 1 to 2-inch flowers on strong stems. The plants average 3½ feet tall and bloom very profusely.

8695 Mary Munns. Finest pure lavender. 40c each; 3 to 9, 35c each.

8691 Tip Top. Vivid raspberry-red. 40c each; 3 to 9, 35c each.

8694 Yellow Gem. Pure yellow. Best of the yellows. 40c each; 3 to 9, 35c each.

"Dainty Bouquet" Collection
No. 8601

One each of the three Dainty Pompon Dahlias

3 tubers for only **95c**

Separately packed and labeled. Mailing weight 1 lb.

MINIATURE DAHLIAS
8686 **Coralette**
8689 **Little Roseatta**   8679 **Bishop of Llandaff**

All Are No. 1 Grade, Clean Bulbs

WHITE AND CREAM

8731 Leading Lady. (90 days.) Most popular cream sport of Picardy. 1 to 9, 12c each; 10 to 49, 11c each; 50 to 99, 10c each.

8716 Margaret Beaton. (85 days.) Snow-white with a red blotch in the throat. 1 to 9, 8c eac .; .0 to 49, 7c each; 50 to 99, 6c each.

8722 Silver Wings. (90 days.) Giant, wide-open blooms of unmarked white, slightly ruffled and well placed on a long straight spike. 1 to 9, 20c each; 10 to 49, 18c each; 50 to 99, 16c each.

ORANGE

8733 Holland's Glory. Large, beautiful salmon-orange with yellow throat. Tall spikes. An excellent cut flower. 1 to 9, 9c each; 10 to 49, 8c each; 50 to 99, 7c each.

YELLOW

8740 Oregon Gold. (110 days.) A superb light yellow. Large florets on long, straight stems. 1 to 9, 9c each; 10 to 49, 8c each; 50 to 99, 7½c each.

8739 Spotlight. (80 days.) A most outstanding yellow of recent introduction. Smooth deep yellow with a feathered scarlet throat. Long spikes; good grower. 1 to 9, 12c each; 10 to 49, 11c each; 50 to 99, 10c each.

ROSE

8708 Burma. (88 days.) Large, heavily ruffled florets of rich deep rose. 1 to 9, 12c each; 10 to 49, 11c each; 50 to 99, 10c each.

SCARLET AND RED

8773 King Klick. (90 days.) Giant blooms of very bright scarlet. One of the best in its color. 1 to 9, 9c each; 10 to 49, 8c each; 50 to 99, 7c each.

8777 Mansoer. A new outstanding black-red variety from Holland. The very large florets are deep blo d-red with a blackish brown, velvety glow. Opens 7 to 10 florets on a tall tem.   to 9, 9c each; 10 to 49, 8c each; 50 to 99, 7c each.

8769 Red Charm. New popular red. A prize-winner at the shows. 1 to 9, 9c each; 10 to 49, 8c each; 50 to 99, 7c each.

SALMON-PINK

8748 Picardy. (90 days.) Clear, soft shrimp-pink. 1 to 9, 8c each; 10 to 49, 7c each; 50 to 99, 6c each.

PINK

8753 Ethel Cave Cole. (80 days.) Finest new light pink. Opens 7 to 8 florets on a 26-inch flower head. 1 to 9, 8c each; 10 to 49, 7c each; 50 to 99, 6c each.

8756 Greta Garbo. (85 days.) Buds of soft salmon-rose open to delicate pink and rosy buff. 1 to 9, 8c each; 10 to 49, 7c each; 50 to 99, 6c each.

LAVENDER

8779 Elizabeth the Queen. (86 days.) Ruffled flowers of clear lavender with darker lines in the throat. 1 to 9, 12c each; 10 to 49, 11c each; 50 to 99, 10c each.

PURPLE

8790 Purple Supreme. (95 days.) Deep purple with lighter edge. The favorite in its class. 1 to 9, 8c each; 10 to 49, 7c each; 50 to 99, 6c each.

LIGHT VIOLET

8784 Blue Beauty. Early midseason. The best light blue. 1 to 9, 8c each; 10 to 49, 7c each; 50 to 99, 6c each.

SMOKY

8796 High Finance. An attractive combination of smoky grays and tans with tints of orange and a cream throat. 1 to 9, 12c each; 10 to 49, 11c each; 50 to 99, 10c each.

MIXED

8798 P.-W.'s Superb Mixed. Our special mixture well blended from the best named types. 1 to 9, 6c each; 10 to 49, 5c each; 50 to 99, 4½c each.

Gladiolus are among the most popular of all summer-flowering bulbs because they come in such rich colors, are so easily grown and make such superb cut flowers. Not at all particular as to soil and exposure, the bulbs may be planted in rows by themselves, for cutting purposes, or they may very well be massed in groups in the shrub border or among perennials. Set the corms 3 to 6 inches deep, according to their size and the texture of the soil.

8773
KING
KLICK

The Glamoro

8820
POINSETTIA
$1.00 each

8844
**MME. JOS.
PERRAUD**
$1.00 each

8876
PINK DAWN
$1.00 each

8810
ETOILE DE HOLLANDE
$1.00 each

8836
**DUQUESA
DE PENARANDA**
$1.00 each

8888 MME. JULES BOUCHE $1.00 each

8856
MRS. E. P. THOM
$1.00 each

8866
EDITH NELLIE PERKINS
$1.00 each

8806
CHRISTOPHER
STONE
$1.00 each

8960 **TAFFETA**
Pat. 716
$1.50 each

8909 **FORTY-NINER**
Pat. 792
$2.00 each

5
Modern
ROSES

COLLECTION No. 8928

Each of the Roses on this page is a recent All-America Selection—each a winner in its color class.

Save $1.40 on the purchase of this Modern Rose group. One of each illustrated on this page (a $9.00 value)

ONLY **$7.60**

Mailing weight 8 lbs.

8946 **PEACE** ©
Pat. 591
$2.00 each

8940 **NOCTURNE**
Pat. 713
$1.50 each

8959 **TALLYHO**
Pat. 828
$2.00 each

34

The Big Four for 1950

ALL-AMERICA WINNERS

COLLECTION No. 8926

Here are four really wonderful Roses, judged superior in two-year tests in every section of the United States. Two of them also won Gold Medal awards in famous European trials.

You save $1.50 when you purchase the group of four husky plants. (A $9.50 value)   Only **$8.00**

Mailing weight 7 lbs.

8936 **MISSION BELLS**
Pat. Applied for
$2.50 each

8955 **SUTTER'S GOLD**
Pat. Applied for
$2.50 each

© 9005 **FASHION. $2.00 each. Floribunda, 18 inches tall.**
Pat. 789.

8901 **CAPISTRANO**
Pat. Applied for
$2.50 each

35

8902 **CRIMSON GLORY.** Pat. 105.

© 8900 **COUNTESS VANDAL.** Pat. 38.

8956 **Show Girl.** Pat. 646. A strong, upright grower, branching freely and producing a constant supply of amazing long, intense pink buds. Pleasing fragrance. $1.50 each; 3 or more, $1.25 each.

8957 **Signora.** Pat. 201. Buds of warm brownish orange open to lighter mandarin and salmon. Signora is a tall, vigorous grower with glossy, dark green foliage, in many respects superior to the well-known President Herbert Hoover. Very fragrant. 2½ to 3 feet tall. $1.35 each; 3 or more, $1.12 each.

MINIATURE ROSES

8994 **ROSA ROULETTI.** Rose-pink, double flowers. 8 inches tall.

8995 **TOM THUMB.** Pat. 169. Perfectly formed, tiny roses of rich crimson.

Each of above, 85c each; 3 or more, 75c each

36

Novelty ROSES

8898 **Charlotte Armstrong.** Pat. 455. AARS. Long-stemmed flowers are spectrum-red in the cooler seasons and cerise-red during the summer. They open slowly and retain their beauty a long time. $1.50 each; 3 to 29, $1.25 each.

8900 **Countess Vandal.** Pat. 38. One of the most widely planted Roses. Long, tapered buds of salmon-pink, shaded copper and gold. 2 to 2½ feet tall. $1.35 each; 3 to 29, $1.12 each.

8902 **Crimson Glory.** Pat. 105. Its large, shapely, fragrant buds open into full double blooms of deep vivid crimson. A continuous bloomer and an outstanding Rose in every respect. $1.35 each; 3 to 29, $1.12 each.

8904 **Debonair.** Pat. 677. A handsome plant with vigorous upright habit and glossy, dark green foliage. Outstanding for its tightly curled buds and graceful, high-centered flower. Buds of rich citron-yellow open to deep primrose; fragrant. $1.50 each; 3 to 29, $1.25 each.

8908 **Eclipse.** Pat. 172. One of the all-time great Roses, and one which grows well in all localities. Long, streamlined buds of pale yellow. 2 to 2½ feet tall. $1.35 each; 3 to 29, $1.12 each.

8914 **Heart's Desire.** Pat. 501. AARS. A popular red Rose with long pointed buds. The large petals of fine substance last for a long time. Fragrant. $1.50 each; 3 to 29, $1.25 each.

8922 **Lowell Thomas.** Pat. 595. AARS. One of the best lemon-yellow Roses. The 25-petaled blooms open from beautiful buds with high-cupped centers, the petals rolling outward to make magnificent, glowing flowers over 4 inches across when fully open. Plants sturdily upright, with good foliage. $1.50 each; 3 to 29, $1.25 each.

8934 **Mirandy.** Pat. 632. AARS. A plant of tall, vigorous habit, producing large, double blooms of rich maroon-red with penetrating fragrance. $1.50 each; 3 to 29, $1.25 each.

8939 **Mme. Henri Guillot.** Pat. 337. Fragrant, urn-shaped buds of raspberry-pink opening to flame-red. A vigorous grower with large, shiny foliage. $1.50 each; 3 to 29, $1.25 each.

8941 **New Yorker.** Pat. 823. Large blooms of rich velvety scarlet with stimulating fragrance. The plants are bushy and vigorous, with lots of flowers. $2.00 each; 3 to 29, $1.67 each.

8949 **Rex Anderson.** Pat. 335. One of the few highly dependable white Roses. The perfectly formed, delicate ivory-white flowers, which open slowly, are large and fully double. Vigorous and free blooming. 2 feet tall. $1.50 each; 3 to 29, $1.25 each.

8947 **Rubaiyat.** Pat. 758. AARS. The gorgeous tapered buds of rich cerise-red, deeper as the flower expands, are delicately fragrant. A vigorous grower and persistent bloomer. $1.50 each; 3 or more, $1.25 each.

8951 **San Fernando.** Pat. 785. AARS. A perfectly shaped, streamlined bud of intensely brilliant red and a rich heady perfume are the outstanding characteristics of this All-America Selection. The petals of glowing currant-red, changing to bright scarlet, have a firm heavy texture that gives them a long-lasting quality. $2.00 each; 3 or more, $1.67 each.

8957
SIGNORA.
Pat. 201.

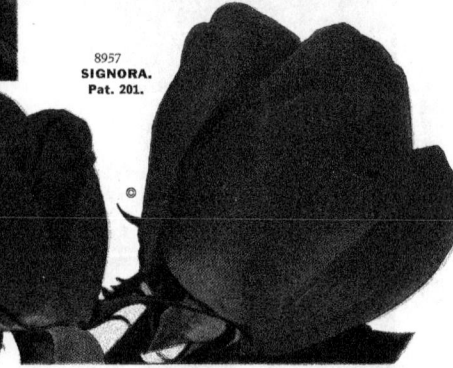

CRIMSON AND SCARLET

Grenoble. Glorious deep crimson-red.
McGredy's Scarlet. Dark rose-scarlet flowers of large size.
Red Talisman. With the perfect bud form of Talisman, this right-growing Rose is one of the best reds.

PINK

Dainty Bess. Large, single, rose-pink blooms with wine-d stamens.
Editor McFarland. Perfectly formed, fresh deep pink.
Picture. Warm pink with undertones of salmon. A inty flower of exquisite form.
The Doctor. Long, pointed buds and enormous blooms silvery pink. Fragrant.

WHITE AND BLUSH-WHITE

McGredy's Ivory. Large, well-shaped, creamy white, fragrant.
Pedralbes. Large, 5-inch, long-stemmed blooms of unique aterlily form. Long buds of pale lemon-yellow, changing to eamy white and finally to pure white.

8858
SOEUR THERESE

*See pages 32
and 33 for other
$1.00 Roses.*

8812
GRENOBLE

YELLOW

8851 **Golden Dawn.** A lovely, well-formed flower of sunflower-yellow changing to lemon. A vigorous grower and a profuse bloomer. Fragrant.
8854 **Joanna Hill.** Buds of orange-yellow opening to double flowers of orange and cream.
8859 **McGredy's Yellow.** Lovely bud and flower of bright buttercup-yellow.
8858 **Soeur Therese.** Fine long, pointed, yellow buds with scarlet veining. Fragrant.

COPPER-SALMON

8832 **Autumn.** Rich burnt-orange, yellow and red.
8834 **Girona.** Richly fragrant flowers of soft golden yellow with a collar of Tyrian-rose.
8839 **Mrs. Sam McGredy.** Very rich copper-orange, heavily flushed with Lincoln red. Fragrant.
8848 **Talisman.** Sensational rich golden apricot, stained copper.

All above Everblooming Roses, $1.00 each; 3 to 29 of one variety, 93c each; 30 or more of one variety, 84c each

Shrub ROSES

These form an appropriate background for the Hybrid Tea Rose garden and combine well with other shrubs in a border

HYBRID PERPETUALS

4 **American Beauty.** Carmine-red.
8 **American Beauty, White (Frau Karl Druschki).** igorous grower.
0 **Paul Neyron.** A thornless bush with gigantic pink flowers. ragrant.

RUGOSA

The Rugosas are a distinct class having dark green, very deeply wrinkled leaves and double flowers with short ruffled petals.
8976 **F. J. Grootendorst, Red.** Red flowers in clusters. 3 to 4 feet tall.

SWEETBRIERS

4 **Austrian Copper.** Bright coppery red, the reverse of the petals golden yellow. 6 to 7 feet tall.
5 **Harison's Yellow.** Large, double, yellow flowers in long graceful sprays. 7 to 9 feet tall.
6 **Rosa Hugonis.** Delicate yellow, single flowers on long, arching sprays early in May. 6 to 7 feet tall.

Each of above Shrub Roses, $1.00 each; 3 to 29, 93c each; 30 or more, 84c each

9030 BLAZE. Pat. 10

Everblooming
CLIMBING ROSES

9030 Blaze. Pat. 10. Everblooming form of Paul's Scarlet. $1.50 each; 3 to 29, $1.25 each.

9055 Cl. Crimson Glory. Pat. 736. Deep crimson, fragrant flowers. $2.00 each; 3 to 29, $1.67 each.

9056 Cl. Etoile de Hollande. Flowers identical to the bush form. $1.25 each.

9064 Cl. Heart's Desire. Pat. 663. Large, deep red flowers in great quantity. $1.50 each; 3 to 29, $1.25 each.

9070 Cl. McGredy's Ivory. Same as the bush form. $1.25 each.

9080 Cl. Mrs. E. P. Thom. Good buds of rich yellow; fragrant. $1.25 each; 3 to 29, $1.15 each; 30 to 100, $1.05 each.

9082 Cl. Mrs. Sam McGredy. Pat. 394. Long-stemmed flowers of rich coppery orange. $1.50 each; 3 to 29, $1.25 each.

9086 Cl. Picture. Pat. 524. Clear rose-pink, long-stemmed flowers. Fragrant. $1.50 each; 3 to 29, $1.25 each.

9090 Cl. Pres. Herbert Hoover. Same flower as the bush form. $1.25 each; 3 to 29, $1.15 each.

9047 Cl. Southport. Beautiful long-pointed buds of brilliant scarlet. The flower opens full and cup shaped. Fragrant. $1.25 each; 3 or more, $1.15 each.

9098 Cl. Talisman. Flowers same as bush form; outstanding. $1.25 each.

9067 Dr. J. H. Nicolas. Pat. 457: Large, deep rose-pink. Outstanding performance. $1.50 each.

9068 Mermaid. Single flowers of pale yellow with a gold center. $1.25 each.

9041 New Dawn. Long-stemmed, double, blush-pink blooms; slightly fragrant. $1.25 each; 3 or more, $1.15 each.

HARDY CLIMBING ROSES

9036 American Beauty. Deep rose-pink; fragrant.

9034 Crimson Rambler. Large clusters of scarlet flowers.

9044 Paul's Lemon Pillar. Pale lemon buds and light yellow fragrant flowers.

9042 Paul's Scarlet Climber. Vivid scarlet.

9048 Silver Moon. Large, pure white flowers.

Each of above, $1.00 each; 3 to 29, 93c each; 30 to 100, 84c each

38   9080   CL. MRS. E. P. THOM   9055 CL. CRIMSON GLORY. Pat. 736

Floribunda ROSES

These are extra hardy, everblooming varieties specially bred for mass planting. They are not only permanent but are colorful and beautiful. Plant about 16 inches apart each way.

9026 Cecile Brunner. The "Sweetheart" Rose. Perfect for boutonnieres. Dainty seashell-pink; delightfully fragrant. 18 to 24 inches tall. 2 yr., No. 1, $1.00 each; 3 to 29, 93c each; 30 or more, 84c each.

9002 Chatter. Pat. 739. Remarkably long-lasting clusters of bright crimson flowers 2½ to 3 inches across. The petals are firm textured, holding their color for several days. Almost continuously in bloom. $1.25 each; 3 or more, $1.05 each.

9006 Dagmar Spaeth. A true white sport of Lafayette bearing flowers of the same lovely form. 18 to 24 inches tall. 2 yr., No. 2, 75c each; 3 to 29, 66c each; 30 or more, 60c each.

9012 Else Poulsen. Lasting, brilliant, two-toned rose-pink. Semi-double, sweetly scented. 2½ to 3 feet tall. 2 yr., No. 2, 75c each; 3 to 29, 66c each; 30 or more, 60c each.

9013 Eutin. Extremely large clusters of glowing deep red blooms. Large, mildew-resistant foliage. Vigorous. 75c each; 3 to 29, 66c each; 30 or more, 60c each.

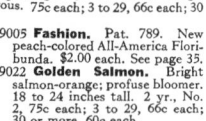

9005 Fashion. Pat. 789. New peach-colored All-America Floribunda. $2.00 each. See page 35.

9022 Golden Salmon. Bright salmon-orange; profuse bloomer. 18 to 24 inches tall. 2 yr., No. 2, 75c each; 3 to 29, 66c each; 30 or more, 60c each.

9018 Improved Lafayette. Medium-sized, deep glowing red flowers suffused with vivid crimson. 18 to 24 inches tall. 2 yr., No. 2, 75c each; 3 to 29, 66c each; 30 or more, 60c each.

9019 Pinkie. Pat. 712. All-America winner. A baby Rose unusually perfect in form. The pink buds are long and slender; the open flower about 2 inches across. 24 inches tall. $1.50 each; 3 or more, $1.25 each.

Five Charming Floribundas

COLLECTION NO. 8932

One each of the five illustrated on this page (a $6.00 value)

Only $5.00

Mailing weight 7 lbs.

© **9016 PINOCCHIO.** Pat. 484
$1.25 each; 3 to 29, $1.05 each

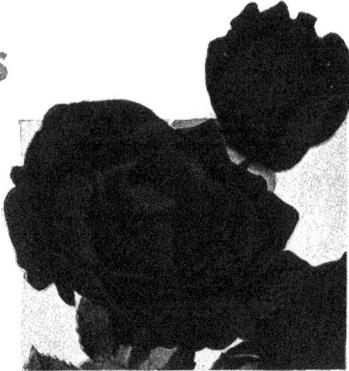

© **9017 WORLD'S FAIR.** Pat. 362
$1.25 each; 3 to 29, $1.05 each

© **9015 GOLDILOCKS.** Pat. 672
$1.50 each; 3 to 29, $1.25 each

9014 FLORADORA
75c each; 3 to 29, 66c each; 30 or more, 60c each

© **9009 DONALD PRIOR.** Pat. 377
$1.25 each; 3 to 29, $1.05 each

39

Flowering Trees

These ornamental trees are a wonderful addition to any planting, for their early spring blooms seem to be a personification of spring itself.

9660 JAPANESE FLOWERING CHERRY
See opposite page

FLOWERING PEACH
See opposite page

9614 ORCHID-FLOWERING ACACIA
See opposite page

9574 FLOWERING CRAB, HOPA
See opposite page

40

Ornamental SHADE TREES

NATURE'S OWN AIR-CONDITIONERS
THE FIRST ESSENTIAL FOR LANDSCAPING THE HOME

NURSERY STOCK	SHIPPING WEIGHT—ORNAMENTAL TREES						
All trees and other nursery stock are priced f.o.b. Salt Lake City. Orders for deciduous nursery stock can be shipped at any time during the spring so long as the plants are dormant. **Early plantings give best results.**	Size	3–4 ft.	4–5 ft.	5–6 ft.	6–8 ft.	8–10 ft.	10–12 ft.
	One tree	5 lbs.	7 lbs.	9 lbs.	12 lbs.	17 lbs.	20 lbs.
	Each additional tree	2 lbs.	3 lbs.	5 lbs.	8 lbs.	10 lbs.	12 lbs.
	Express or Motor Freight recommended for all trees larger than 3–4 ft.						

ACACIA

★*Note.* This group is illustrated on the preceding color page (40).

9614 Orchid-flowering. H 35. A beautiful tree with ★long compound leaves and clusters of deep orchid-pink flowers in June. A medium fast grower. 7 to 8 ft., $4.00 each; 8 to 10 ft., $4.50 each.

Malus · FLOWERING CRABAPPLE

Because of their good growing habits, foliage, flowers and fruits, the Flowering Crabapples are among the best-loved small trees. Very hardy.

9565 Bechtel's. H 12. A very symmetrically formed tree with large, double pink flowers. 3 to 4 ft., $2.00 each; 4 to 5 ft., $2.50 each.

9568 Eleyi. H 15. A mass of red bloom. Dark red fruit that makes fine jelly. 3 to 4 ft., $2.00 each; 5 to 6 ft., $2.50 each.

9578 Floribunda Scheideckeri. H 15. Large, semi-double, pink flowers and yellow fruit. 3 to 4 ft., $2.00 each; 5 to 6 ft., $2.50 each.

9574 Hopa. H 12. A gorgeous mass of soft rose-red, ★single flowers. The tree is upright and uniform in habit. 3 to 4 ft., $2.00 each; 5 to 6 ft., $2.50 each.

9579 Sargenti. H 6–8. A unique variety of low, shrub-like form. The white flowers with yellow anthers are followed by scarlet fruits in the fall. 3 to 4 ft., $2.00 each.

Prunus · FLOWERING CHERRY

9660 Kwanzan. H 25. Large double pink flowers. 2 to ★3 ft., $1.25 each; 3 to 4 ft., $2.00 each; 4 to 6 ft., $3.00 each.

9664 Weeping Single Pink. Slender, graceful, weeping branches. No. 1 heads on 5-ft. standards. $5.00 each.

9684 Sophora japonica

9540 BETULA pendula gracilis (Cutleaf Weeping Birch)

Amygdalus persica · FLOWERING PEACH

9642 Helen Borschers. H 15. Double pink flowers. ★3 to 4 ft., $1.50 each; 4 to 6 ft., $1.75 each.

9644 Double Red. H 15. 3 to 4 ft., $1.50 each; 4 to 6 ft., ★$1.75 each.

Acer · MAPLE

9624 Platanoides. Norway Maple. H 60. A thrifty, clean, hardy species adaptable to almost any soil or climate. Large, attractive leaves, giving ample shade. An ideal street tree enduring city life well. 8 to 10 ft., $3.75 each; 10 to 12 ft., $4.75 each; 2 to 2½-in. caliper, $10.00 each.

9626 Platanoides Schwedleri. Schwedler Maple. H 60. Red and purple foliage in spring, turning golden yellow in autumn. Same habit of growth as Norway Maple. 6 to 8 ft., $4.50 each.

9628 Saccharinum. Silver Maple. H 60. A large, fast-growing tree. 6 to 8 ft., $3.00 each.

Aesculus · HORSE-CHESTNUT

9696 White-flowering. H 60. Magnificent spikes of white flowers, sweetly scented. 6 to 8 ft., $4.50 each.

9543 BETULA, Birch Clumps, European White

Betula · BIRCH

9542 **Pendula.** European White Birch. A tall, distinctive, white-barked tree of upright form. The leaves are nearly round but abruptly pointed. 6 to 8 ft., $3.00 each.

9540 **Pendula gracilis.** Cutleaf Weeping Birch. White branches with hanging, slender stems and deeply cut leaves. Very beautiful, hardy and clean. Plant very early to insure a good start. Special handling makes these trees available for February planting. The trunks of smooth-barked trees like Birch should be wrapped for the first year after planting. 7 to 8 ft., $4.00 each; 8 to 10 ft., $4.50 each.

9543 **Birch Clumps, European White.** H 35. Especially useful for naturalistic effects. 6 to 7 ft., $4.00 each.

Cercis · REDBUD

9562 **Canadensis.** H 30. Striking, ornamental trees with pea-shaped, pink flowers in early spring before the leaves appear. 4 to 5 ft., $2.50 each.

Crataegus · FLOWERING HAWTHORN

9600 **Paul's Double Scarlet.** H 15. Crimson-scarlet flowers followed by large red berries. 5 to 6 ft., $3.00 each; 7 to 8 ft., $4.50 each.

CATALPA

9558 **Speciosa.** Western Catalpa. Very large leaves and large clusters of white flowers in spring. 8 to 10 ft., $2.00 each.

Elaeagnus angustifolia · RUSSIAN OLIVE

9638 H 20. Silvery green foliage. Very hardy and vigorous. Valuable for screens, hedges and as a color accent. 5 to 6 ft., $1.50 each; 8 to 10 ft., $2.50 each.

42

Fraxinus · ASH

9548 **Pennsylvanica lanceolata.** Green Ash. H 50. Shapely, round top with dark green foliage. 6 to 8 ft., $2.50 each; 8 to 10 ft., $3.00 each; 10 to 12 ft., $4.50 each.

MALE ASH TREES

The absence of the seasonal litter of seeds and the resulting crop of troublesome seedlings accounts for the widespread use of these specially propagated trees. In addition, the foliage of male trees is more abundant, more glossy and luxuriant.

9554 **Male Excelsior.** H 75. The broad head and abundant glossy foliage make it one of the most desirable of all Ash trees. 6 to 8 ft., $3.50 each; 8 to 10 ft., $4.50 each; 10 to 12 ft., $6.00 each.

9550 **Male Green.** H 50–60. A tall, pyramidal tree with rounded head. 6 to 8 ft., $3.50 each; 8 to 10 ft., $4.50 each; 10 to 12 ft., $6.00 each.

Laburnum Vossi · GOLDEN-CHAIN

9602 A small tree with flowers of pure golden yellow in 18-inch clusters. 5 to 6 ft., $3.50 each.

Morus · MULBERRY

9636 **Kingan.** Fruitless Mulberry. H 25. A clean, fast-growing tree with large leaves. 6 to 8 ft., $3.00 each.

9634 **Tatarica.** Russian Mulberry. H 25. Another quick grower. 6 to 8 ft., $1.50 each.

9632 **Tea's Weeping.** H 15. An ideal dwarf, weeping tree for planting in feature positions. The composite of thick, arched branches, rough brown bark and large, deeply wrinkled leaves is a picture of rugged charm. 1-yr. heads, $4.50 each.

Platanus · PLANE-TREE

9646 **Acerifolia.** London Plane-tree. H 70. Forms a fine, spreading, well-rounded head. Leaves are large and deeply lobed. 5 to 6 ft., $2.50 each; 8 to 10 ft., $3.50 each.

9550 ASH, Male Green

PORTER-WALTON COMPANY

Populus · POPLAR

9650 **Bolleana.** H 60. A tall, columnar tree. Silvery foliage. 6 to 8 ft., $2.50 each; 8 to 10 ft., $3.00 each.

9652 **Canadian.** H 60. A sturdy, rapid-growing tree. 6 to 8 ft., $1.50 each; 8 to 10 ft., $2.00 each.

9654 **Canadensis.** Carolina Poplar. H 50. Branching habit. 6 to 8 ft., $1.50 each; 8 to 10 ft., $2.00 each.

9656 **Nigra italica.** Lombardy Poplar. H 80. Narrow and columnar. 6 to 8 ft., $1.50 each; 8 to 10 ft., $2.00 each.

Prunus · FLOWERING PLUM

9678 **Double Triloba.** See page 47.

9672 **Newport.** H 15. Single light pink flowers. 4 to 5 ft., $1.50 each.

9676 **Thundercloud.** The best and darkest foliage of all the purple-leaved Flowering Plums. Single, light pink flowers. 2 to 3 ft., $1.00 each; 3 to 4 ft., $1.50 each.

Gleditsia · LOCUST

9616 **Thornless Honeylocust.** H 50. Very small foliage. An ideal lawn tree. 5 to 6 ft., $1.75 each; 7 to 8 ft., $2.50 each.

Salix · WILLOW

9690 **Weeping Babylonian.** H 30. Green bark. 5 to 6 ft., $1.75 each; 6 to 8 ft., $2.50 each; 8 to 10 ft. $3.00 each.

9698 **Weeping Golden.** H 25. Golden bark. 5 to 6 ft., $1.75 each; 6 to 8 ft., $2.50 each.

Sophora japonica
CHINESE SCHOLAR-TREE

9684 H 60. A symmetrical, round-headed tree with glossy, dark green foliage. Cream-colored panicles of bloom appear in late July. 5 to 6 ft., $3.50 each; 6 to 8 ft., $4.00 each.

Sorbus · MOUNTAIN-ASH

9552 **Aucuparia.** European Mountain-Ash. H 45. White flower-clusters 5 inches across, followed by orange-red berries. 6 to 8 ft., $3.00 each.

9676 PRUNUS, Thundercloud

Ulmus · ELM

9592 **Moline.** H 75. Columnar form. Older specimens are more spreading. 6 to 8 ft., $3.00 each.

9584 **Parvifolia.** Chinese Elm. H 40. Open-headed tree with small, firm leaves, shining above and smooth underneath. 5 to 6 ft., $1.25 each; 6 to 8 ft., $1.50 each; 8 to 10 ft., $2.50 each; 10 to 12 ft., $3.00 each.

NUT TREES *Beautiful and Fruitful*

9716 **Almond, Northern.** H 20. Exceptionally hardy and productive, bearing soft-shelled nuts of excellent quality. 3 to 4 ft., $2.00 each; 4 to 6 ft., $2.50 each.

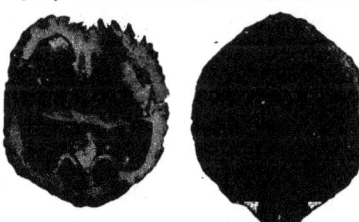

9732 WALNUT, Improved Thomas Black

9720 **Almond, Utah I.X.L.** H 20. Smooth, soft-shelled nuts of fine flavor. 3 to 4 ft., $2.00 each; 4 to 6 ft., $2.50 each.

9724 **Filbert, Barcelona.** This is the leading commercial variety and one of the best croppers, producing large round nuts. It needs one or more pollinators for best results. 3 to 4 ft., $2.00 each.

9727 **Filbert, Daviana.** Produces medium-sized nuts of fine quality and is a fair bearer. Fine for pollinizing Barcelona. 3 to 4 ft., $2.00 each.

9728 **Walnut, English.** Hardy strain. 6 to 8 ft., $4.00 each.

9732 **Walnut, Improved Thomas Black.** H 80. Large nuts with large kernels which come out in halves. Has a distinctive Walnut flavor. The tree is fast growing, upright, and begins bearing in five years. 6 to 7 ft., $4.00 each.

EVERGREENS

All evergreens are quoted f.o.b. Salt Lake City. Most sizes are too large and heavy for parcel post and must therefore be shipped by freight or express.

ARBORVITAE (Thuja)

9476 Orientalis excelsa. Western Arborvitae. This excellent variety, which is native in Western America, has the richest, most luxuriant green color of all the Arborvitae. It is of broad conical habit, is a rapid grower, and very beautiful either in its natural form or closely trimmed as a formal specimen.
In gal. cans, 1 to 9, $1.50 each; 10 to 29, $1.30 each.
15 to 18 in., $3.50 each; 18 to 24 in., $4.50 each.

9478 Occidentalis elegantissima. Gold-tip Arborvitae. Sturdy, compact trees. 2 to 2½ ft., $6.50 each.

9474 Orientalis elegantissima. Gold-tinged Column Arborvitae. Tall, pyramidal evergreen. 18 to 24 in., $4.50 each; 3 to 4 ft., $10.00 each; 4 to 5 ft., $12.50 each.

Dwarf Varieties

9482 Occidentalis Douglasi aurea. Distinct color contrasts are created by including this bright bronzy yellow tree in your plantings of other evergreens. It is broad and pyramidal in growth, with flattened, irregularly curled foliage. 30 to 36 in., $7.50 each; 3 to 4 ft., $10.00 each; 4 to 5 ft., $12.50 each.

9488 Orientalis aurea nana. Berckman's Dwarf Ever-golden Arborvitae. The most wanted Arborvitae. Dwarf, golden tipped, pyramidal. Always shapely and beautiful.
In gal. cans, 1 to 9, $1.50 each.
12 to 15 in., $2.75 each; 15 to 18 in., $3.75 each.

9484 Orientalis meldensis. Neat, pyramidal form with deep green foliage.
In gal. cans, $1.50 each.
12 to 15 in., $2.75 each; 15 to 18 in., $3.75 each.

9462 JUNIPER, chinensis pyramidalis

9476 ARBORVITÆ orientalis excelsa

PYRAMIDAL AND NOVELTY JUNIPERS

9469 Chinensis Keteleeri. Dark green. Best variety for shade. 30 to 36 in., $7.50 each; 3 to 4 ft., $10.00 each.

9462 Chinensis pyramidalis. Rich blue-green.
In gal. cans, 1 to 9, $1.50 each; 10 to 29, $1.30 each.

9464 Scopulorum. Colorado Juniper. Compact, columnar growth from a single central stem. It is of unusual silver-blue color. 30 to 36 in., $7.50 each; 3½ to 4 ft., $10.00 each; 4 to 5 ft., $12.50 each.

9470 Virginiana. Red Cedar. Lustrous bluish green foliage turning purplish red in late fall and winter. 3 to 4 ft., $10.00 each; 4 to 5 ft., $12.50 each; 5 to 6 ft., $16.00 each.

9466 Virginiana Cannarti. Deep rich green; fine textured. 3 to 4 ft., $10.00 each; 4 to 5 ft., $12.50 each.

9453 Pfitzer Pyramids. Trimmed to upright form. 2½ to 3 ft., $10.00 each.

9461 Silver-Blue Globe Junipers. Trimmed to formal shape. 18 to 24 in., $7.50 each.

NOTE: Yearly trimming of Junipers and Arborvitae is very beneficial, making sturdier, more compact trees that sustain less winter snow damage. Also very important is the fact that the plants may be kept at any desired size. In the Mountain States trimming should be done in early spring. Ask for our free folder—"How to handle Evergreens".

PORTER-WALTON COMPANY

SPREADING JUNIPERS

9450 **Chinensis Pfitzeriana.** Pfitzer Juniper. Quick growing. The most widely planted spreading Juniper. In gal. cans, 1 to 9, $1.50 each; 10 to 29, $1.30 each. 15 to 18 in., B&B, $5.25 each; 18 to 24 in., B&B, $6.00 each.

9456 **Chinensis Sargenti Blue.** A very low, creeping form growing only 8 to 12 inches above the ground and spreading 6 to 8 feet. The bright bluish green foliage creates a pleasing contrast with the ordinary green of other plants. In gal. cans, 1 to 9, $1.50 each; 10 to 29, $1.30 each. 15 to 18 in., $5.25 each; 18 to 24 in., $6.00 each.

9452 **Sabina tamariscifolia.** A small, compact grower attaining a spread of only 6 to 7 feet. In gal. cans, 1 to 9, $1.50 each; 10 to 29, $1.30 each. 15 to 18 in., B&B, $6.00 each.

9454 **Sabina, Von Ehron.** Slender, wiry branchlets of semi-spreading habit. 18 to 24 in., $6.00 each.

CONIFERS

Picea · SPRUCE

9510 **Pungens.** Colorado Green Spruce. Tall, stately tree growing 40 feet tall. 15 to 18 in., $4.00 each.

PINUS · Pine

9498 **Mugo.** Dwarf Pine. A low, dense plant of formal habit with bright green leaves. It is best used in entrance or foundation plantings, also as a rock-garden plant or single specimen. It does well in a wide variety of soils and exposures. 12 to 15 in., $3.00 each; 15 to 18 in., $4.00 each; 18 to 24 in., $5.00 each.

9494 **Nigra.** Austrian Pine. A beautiful evergreen shade tree reaching a height of 40 feet. The leaves are borne two in a sheath, straight and slender, from 4 to 5 inches long, and are of deep rich green. Gas and a smoky atmosphere have no effect on its growth. 24 to 30 in., $5.00 each; 3 to 4 ft., $10.00 each; 4 to 5 ft., $12.50 each.

9534 PYRACANTHA coccinea Lalandi

9498 PINE, Mugo

BROAD-LEAVED EVERGREENS

Buxus · BOXWOOD

9520 **Sempervirens.** Dense, glossy foliage. Erect plant. 24 to 30 in., $7.50 each.

COTONEASTER

9522 **Horizontalis.** An ideal dwarf shrub for a partially shaded situation. 18 inches tall. In gal. cans, 1 to 9, $1.50 each; 10 to 29, $1.30 each. 5 gal. cans, $5.00 each.

EUONYMUS

9426 **Fortunei Carrierei.** Glossy Wintercreeper. Fits beautifully into foundation plantings. 3 feet tall. In gal. cans, 1 to 9, $1.50 each; 10 to 29, $1.30 each. 18 to 24 in., B&B, $3.00 each. 2-yr., bare root, 1 to 9, 90c each; 10 to 29, 87c each.

9528 **Japonicus.** Upright habit of growth. Glossy foliage. 8 feet tall. In gal. cans, 1 to 9, $1.50 each; 10 to 29, $1.30 each. 2½ to 3 ft., $6.00 each.

MAHONIA

9530 **Aquifolium.** Oregon Hollygrape. Shiny leaves in attractively changing shades of green. 5 feet tall. In gal. cans, 1 to 9, $1.50 each; 10 to 29, $1.30 each. 15 to 18 in., $3.50 each; 18 to 24 in., heavy field grown, $4.50 each.

PYRACANTHA

9534 **Coccinea Lalandi.** Foliage dark green. Orange-scarlet berries in the fall. 10 feet tall. In gal. cans, 1 to 9, $1.50 each; 10 to 29, $1.30 each. 18 to 24 in., in 3-gal. cans, 1 to 9, $3.00 each; 10 to 29, $2.75 each. 30 to 36 in., in 3-gal. cans, 1 to 9, $3.75 each; 10 to 29, $3.40 each.

9536 **Coccinea pauciflora.** Dwarf Pyracantha. Outstanding for its compact, rounded, formal habit. 6 feet tall. In 3-gal. cans, 1 to 9, $4.50 each; 10 to 29, $3.90 each.

VIBURNUM

9538 **Burkwoodi.** Gardenia-scented Snowball. Waxy, pinkish white flowers; semi-evergreen foliage. 4 feet tall. 24 to 30 in., B&B, $4.50 each.

Beautiful ORNAMENTAL...
and FLOWERING SHRUBS

NOTE: Height and spread are indicated following the name. For example, H 3–4; S 3–4 means Height 3 to 4 feet, Spread 3 to 4 feet.

BERBERIS · Barberry

9204 Mentorensis. Mentor Barberry. Pat. 99. H 3–4; S 3–4. (See page 50.) New hardy, semi-evergreen Barberry. Sturdy, erect growth, making excellent hedges and foundation plants.
15 to 18 in., 1 to 9, 85c each; 10 to 29, 60c each; 30 to 100, 50c each.
18 to 24 in., 1 to 9, $1.00 each; 10 to 29, 80c each; 30 to 100, 70c each.
2 to 2½ ft., 1 to 9, $1.25 each; 10 to 29, $1.00 each; 30 to 100, 90c each.

9206 Thunbergi atropurpurea. Red-leaved Japanese Barberry. H 3–4; S 3–4. Identical with the popular Japanese Barberry except for the foliage, which is rich bronzy red.
15 to 18 in., 1 to 9, 75c each; 10 to 29, 65c each; 30 to 100, 60c each.
18 to 24 in., 1 to 9, 90c each; 10 to 29, 80c each; 30 to 100, 75c each.

Buddleia · BUTTERFLY-BUSH
(See page 49)

9211 Royal Red. Pat. 556. H 5–6. Large sprays of dark royal purple bloom. 2-yr. plants, 90c each.

BUSH CHERRY

9214 Hansen's. H 3–4; S 4–5. Excellent as hedges and ornamental shrubs. 2 to 3 ft., 90c each.

Cydonia · FLOWERING QUINCE

9224 COTONEASTER divaricata

CARAGANA · Pea-Tree

9212 Siberian. H 8–10; S 8. Numerous small clusters of yellow flowers. 2 to 3 ft., hedge size, 30c each; 10 to 29, 25c each; 30 to 100, 20c each.

Caryopteris · BLUE MIST SHRUB

9213 H 2½. Silvery green foliage. Light blue, fringed flowers in late summer. 2-yr. plants, 90c each.

Cornus · DOGWOOD

9218 Sibirica. Red-branched Dogwood. H 6–8; S 6. Cream-colored flowers and light blue fruits, with bright red twigs and branches. 18 to 24 in., 75c each; 2 to 3 ft., 90c each; 3 to 4 ft., $1.25 each.

COTONEASTER

9220 Acutifolia. H 6–7; S 5–6. Glossy green foliage and black berries. 2 to 3 ft., 90c each.
9224 Divaricata. H 5–6; S 4–5. One of our most graceful and beautiful shrubs. Covered in spring with dainty pink flowers and in fall with an abundance of shiny scarlet berries. 2 to 3 ft., bare root, $1.50 each; 2 to 3 ft., B&B, $2.00 each.

EUONYMUS

9242 Alatus compactus. H 5–6; S 5. Foliage bright green, changing to deep rose in autumn. Orange-red berries. 18 to 24 in., $1.50 each.
9244 Americana. H 7–8; S 5–6. A thrifty grower, erect in habit, with deep green foliage and light scarlet fruits which ripen in September. It thrives in partial shade and rather moist soil. 2 to 3 ft., 90c each.

Cydonia · FLOWERING QUINCE

9227 Blood-Red (Rubra grandiflora). Larger and darker flowers than Japanese Scarlet. Blooms earlier. Very fine as a specimen shrub in full sun. 2 to 3 ft., $2.00 each.
9226 Japanese Scarlet. H 4–5; S 5. Brilliant crimson flowers on spiny branches. One of the earliest flowering spring shrubs. 18 to 24 in., 75c each; 2 to 3 ft., 90c each.

Forsythia · GOLDEN BELLS
(See page 49)

9248 Spectabilis. The earliest spring-flowering shrub. Best of all Forsythias. Pure yellow flowers on arching branches. Very easily grown; best when allowed to grow naturally, with practically no pruning. 2 to 3 ft., 90c each; 3 to 4 ft., $1.25 each; 4 to 5 ft., $1.50 each.

46

PORTER-WALTON COMPANY

Hibiscus syriacus · ALTHEA; Rose-of-Sharon

9194 Coelestis. H 10; S 5. Single blue flowers in great quantity. Blooms in late summer. Does well in any well-drained garden soil. 2 to 3 ft., 90c each.

9198 Rubus. H 10; S 5. Large flowers of deep rose-pink with deeper center. Rapid grower, often needing to be cut back. 2 to 3 ft., 90c each.

9196 Snowdrift. H 10; S 5. Giant single, pure white flowers 4 inches across. Very useful in large shrub borders or as a lawn specimen. 2 to 3 ft., 90c each.

HYDRANGEA

9252 Arborescens grandiflora. Hills-of-Snow. H 3; S 3. Heads of snow-white bloom 4 to 5 inches in diameter. Does well in part shade. 2 to 3 ft., $1.50 each.

KERRIA

9270 Japonica, Double. H 4–5; S 3. A graceful shrub with attractive orange-yellow flowers all summer. Foliage turns yellow in autumn. 18 to 24 in., 90c each.

Kolkwitzia amabilis · BEAUTY-BUSH

9272 H 6–8; S 6. Produces an amazing number of pale pink, bell-shaped flowers. 2 to 3 ft., $1.50 each.

Ligustrum · PRIVET

9278 Lodense. Dwarf Privet. H 2–3. Splendid for dwarf shrubs and low hedges.
6 to 8 in., 1 to 9, 35c each; 10 to 29, 28c each; 30 to 100, 25c each.
10 to 12 in., 1 to 9, 40c each; 10 to 29, 35c each; 30 to 100, 32c each.
12 to 18 in., 1 to 9, 45c each; 10 to 29, 40c each; 30 to 100, 38c each.

9276 Obtusifolium Regelianum. Regel's Privet. H 6–8; S 4–5. Horizontal branches with metallic black berries in the fall.
2 to 3 ft., 1 to 9, 90c each; 10 to 29, 80c each.

9274 Vulgare. English Privet. H 10–12. The most popular large hedge plant.
12 to 18 in., 1 to 9, 25c each; 10 to 29, 22c each; 30 to 100, 20c each.
18 to 24 in., 1 to 9, 35c each; 10 to 29, 30c each; 30 to 100, 25c each.

Lonicera · BUSH HONEYSUCKLE

9266 Morrowi. H 6–8; S 6. White and yellow flowers; colorful berries. 2 to 3 ft., 90c each.

9258 Tatarica. Tatarian Honeysuckle. H 8–10; S 6–8. Pink. These Tatarian varieties are the most popular tall Bush Honeysuckles. 2 to 3 ft., 90c each.

9260 Tatarica pulcherrima. H 8–10; S 6–8. Bright red.
12 to 18 in., 1 to 9, 50c each; 10 to 29, 45c each; 30 to 100, 38c each.
2 to 3 ft., 90c each.

9272 KOLKWITZIA amabilis

SEED AND NURSERY SPECIALISTS

9266 Lonicera · BUSH HONEYSUCKLE MORROWI

POTENTILLA

9330 Fruticosa. H 2–3; S 3. Produces an abundance of yellow blooms over a long period. 18 to 24 in., 90c each.

Prunus Amygdalus · FLOWERING ALMOND

9190 Double Pink. H 4–5; S 4. (See page 49.) Sweetly scented flowers before the leaves appear. 18 to 24 in., 75c each; 2 to 3 ft., 90c each.

9192 White. H 5–6. 18 to 24 in., 75c each; 2 to 3 ft., 90c each.

Prunus triloba · FLOWERING PLUM

9678 Double. H 8–10. Many rose-pink blooms in early spring. 3 to 4 ft., $1.50 each.

RHODOTYPOS

9338 Kerrioides. White Kerria. H 4–5; S 5. White flowers followed by black fruits that hang on all winter. Very attractive foliage. 2 to 3 ft., $1.50 each.

Philadelphus · MOCK-ORANGE

9325 Snowflake. Pat. 538. H 10–12. This new double Mock-Orange is truly outstanding. Large, sweetly scented flowers of glistening white on a fast-growing, exceptionally hardy plant. 2 to 3 ft., $1.50 each.

9328 Virginalis. H 7–8; S 7. (See page 49.) A tall, hardy plant with large, double-crested, fragrant white blooms throughout the season. 2 to 3 ft., 90c each.

Rhus · SUMAC

9340 Canadensis. Fragrant Sumac. H 3–4; S 4–5. Yellow, catkin-like flowers. The foliage, unlike that of any other Sumac, is very fragrant when crushed. 18 to 24 in., 90c each.

9342 Glabra. Smooth Sumac. H 6–8; S 3–4. A new cutleaf variety with a fine display of fruit. 3 to 4 ft., 90c each.

Robinia hispida · ROSE ACACIA

9348 H 4–5; S 5. Pea-like, rose-pink flowers. 2 to 3 ft., 90c each.

SHIPPING WEIGHT OF HEDGE PLANTS					
Size	8–10 in.	10–12 in.	12–15 in.	15–18 in.	18–24 in.	2–3 ft.
10 plants	2 lbs.	4	8	10	12	15
25 plants	5 lbs.	8	16	20	25	30
100 plants	15 lbs.	25	50	70	80	100

Syringa · FRENCH LILACS

Syringa · GORGEOUS NEW FRENCH LILACS

Grown on their own roots, adapted to intermountain climate; H 10–18.
Lilacs are best planted from late October until the ground freezes, but very early spring planting will also give good results.
D indicates double blooms; S, single.

9284 **Charles Joly.** D. Long-lasting blooms of dark purplish red. 2 to 3 ft., $1.75 each.
9294 **Ellen Willmott.** D. Immense panicles of perfectly formed, creamy white flowers. 18 to 24 in., $2.00 each; 2 to 3 ft., $3.00 each.
9281 **Clark's Giant.** S. Pat. 754. No other Lilac can match this new giant for size of the individual florets nor its tremendous panicles. The buds are soft pinkish mauve opening to rich sky-blue florets 1 to 1½ inches across. The bush, too, is exceptionally vigorous and erect in growth, with very large leaves. 2 to 3 ft., $4.00 each.
9290 **Marechal Lannes.** D. Carmine buds open to large florets of clear violet-blue. This strong grower and late bloomer is one of the best available. 18 to 24 in., $1.25 each; 2 to 3 ft., $1.75 each.
9300 **Pres. Grevy.** D. One of the best double clear blue Lilacs. 18 to 24 in., $1.25 each; 2 to 3 ft., $1.75 each.
9308 **Souv. de Ludwig Spaeth.** S. Very popular. Buds carmine, opening rose-purple. 18 to 24 in., $1.25 each; 2 to 3 ft., $1.75 each.

Lilac Species

9314 **New Chinensis (rothomagensis).** H 10. A distinct sort with slender stems and reddish purple flowers. 15 to 18 in., 1 to 9, 60c each; 10 to 29, 55c each; 30 to 100, 50c each.
2 to 3 ft., 90c each.
9316 **Persica.** Persian Lilac. H 10. Light lilac-purple blooms on slender branches. 2 to 3 ft., 90c each.
9319 **Vulgaris.** Common Purple Lilac. 2 to 3 ft., 90c each.

Sorbaria · FALSE-SPIREA

9358 **Aitchisoni.** H 6–8; S 6–8. Bright green, fern-like foliage and upright panicles of white flowers, 12 to 20 inches long. 3 to 4 ft., $1.50 each.

SPIRAEA

9360 **Arguta.** H 5; S 5. Sprays of pure white flowers in early April. Fern-like foliage is attractive all summer. 18 to 24 in., 75c each.
9362 **Froebeli.** H 4; S 4. (See page 50.) Deep rosy flowers in June. 18 to 24 in., 75c each.
9364 **Prunifolia.** Double Bridal Wreath. H 6; S 6. One of the best. An upright shrub with double white flowers. 2 to 3 ft., $1.50 each.
9368 **Vanhouttei.** Bridal Wreath. H 6–8; S 6. (See page 50.) Long, arching branches. Clusters of white blooms.
18 to 24 in., 1 to 9, 50c each; 10 to 29, 45c each; 30 to 100, 40c each.
2 to 3 ft., 90c each.

SYMPHORICARPOS

9372 **Chenaulti.** H 4–5; S 5. Dainty rich green foliage and handsome red fruit. 2 to 3 ft., 50c each.
9374 **Racemosus.** Snowberry. H 4–5; S 4. (See page 50.) A graceful shrub planted chiefly for its waxy white fruit.
18 to 24 in., 30c each; 10 to 29, 25c each.
2 to 3 ft., 50c each.

TAMARIX

9378 **Hispida.** H 15; S 6. Fern-like foliage. Soft pink flowers in sprays, produced in early spring and again in July. Prune branches to the ground when planting. 2 to 3 ft., 90c each.

VIBURNUM

9384 **Americanum.** Cranberry-shrub. H 10–12; S 10. Large panicles of white flowers followed by bright scarlet fruits. 2 to 3 ft., $1.50 each.
9386 **Dentatum.** Arrow-Wood. H 6–8; S 6. Creamy white flowers and blue-black berries. Foliage is purplish red. 2 to 3 ft., $1.50 each.
9388 **Opulus sterile.** Common Snowball. H 8–10; S 10. Ball-like, pure white flowers in May. 2 to 3 ft., $1.50 each.

WEIGELA

9396 **Bristol Ruby.** Pat. 492. H 5; S 5. The hardiest and most vigorous variety. Flowers are ruby-red to garnet-crimson. 2 to 3 ft., $1.50 each.

9396 WEIGELA, Bristol Ruby

PORTER-WALTON COMPANY

9211 **BUDDLEIA, ROYAL RED.** Pat. 556
2-yr. plants, 90c each

GOLDEN BELL
FORSYTHIA

9248 **FORSYTHIA SPECTABILIS**
2 to 3 ft., 90c each; 3 to 4 ft., $1.25 each

9190 **FLOWERING ALMOND**
18 to 24 in., 75c each; 2 to 3 ft., 90c each

9328 **MOCK-ORANGE, VIRGINALIS.** 2 to 3 ft., 90c each

49

Flower and Berry
SHRUBS

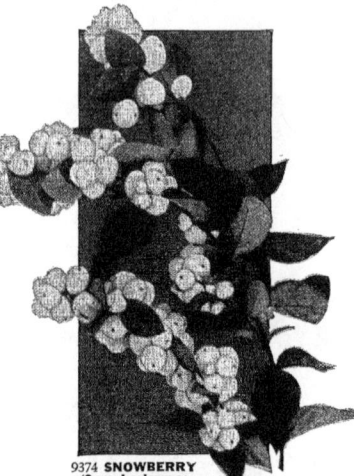

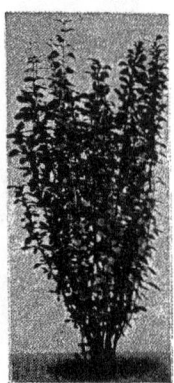

9204 **BERBERIS MENTORENSIS. Pat. 99**
15 to 18 in., 85c each; 18 to 24 in., $1.00 each

FLOWER AND BERRY SHRUBS
COLLECTION No 9163
One each of the four shrubs illustrated on this page,
largest sizes. (A $3.15 value) . . . . . . ONLY **$2.50**
Mailing weight 14 lbs.

9374 **SNOWBERRY**
(**Symphorlcarpos racemosus**)
18 to 24 in., 30c each;
2 to 3 ft., 50c each.

9362 **SPIRAEA FROEBELI**
18 to 24 in., 75c each

9368 **SPIRAEA VANHOUTTEI**
18 to 24 in., 50c each; 2 to 3 ft., 90c each

9421 **CLEMATIS, Ville de Lyon.** 8 to 10 ft. Its many carmine-red blooms with darker tones in the center make a striking display from July until September. Their rich color and texture is rarely equaled in this valuable group. 4-in. pots, staked, $1.50 each.

9416 **CLEMATIS JACKMANI.** 15 ft. Hardy and vigorous in growth, covering itself in summer and early autumn with large, velvety violet-purple flowers. Very popular. 4-in. pots, staked, $1.25 each.

9406 **AMPELOPSIS VEITCHI. Boston Ivy.** Deep green foliage of leathery texture. The vine clings to wood, brick or stone wall surfaces. 3-yr., 90c each. ➤➤➤——

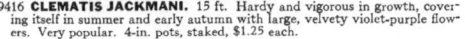

CLIMBERS AND GROUND-COVERS, continued

AMPELOPSIS

9404 Engelmanni. New Virginia Creeper. H 35–40. Self clinging to most surfaces. 2-yr., No. 1, 75c each.

9406 Veitchi. Boston Ivy. See page 51.

Bignonia · TRUMPET-VINE

9408 Mme. Galen. The most striking improvement in this family. Broader trumpets of a beautiful rich shade of orange. 2-yr., $1.25 each.

CLEMATIS

9414 Paniculata. Sweet Autumn Clematis. H 25. A strong-growing but graceful vine. Produces an array of fragrant white flowers from August until fall. 2-yr., dormant, 90c each.

Large-Flowered CLEMATIS

A partially shaded location is ideal for the large-flowered Clematis. They thrive best in a rich loam of rather light texture. The soil should be slightly alkaline and must be well drained. The plants should be set with the collar at least 2 or 3 inches below the surface. A mulch of peat moss to keep the roots moist in summer and protect them in winter is very helpful the first year. See page 51 for illustration and price.

EUONYMUS

9422 Fortunei coloratus. H 1. An evergreen creeper of compact form and luxuriant foliage for ground-cover work. 2-yr., 1 to 9, 90c each; 10 to 29, 80c each; 30 to 100, 75c each.

9424 Radicans vegetus. Evergreen Wintercreeper. H 15. An excellent wall or ground-cover. 2-yr., No. 1, 1 to 9, $1.25 each; 10 to 29, $1.10 each.

Lonicera HONEYSUCKLE

9430 Goldflame. An everblooming Honeysuckle of remarkable beauty. 2-yr., 1 to 9, 90c each; 10 to 29, 80c each; 30 to 100, 75c each.

9432 Japonica Halliana. Hall's Japan Honeysuckle. Semi-evergreen ground-cover or climber. Fragrant white and yellow flowers. 2-yr., 1 to 9, 50c each; 10 to 29, 45c each; 30 to 100, 40c each.

Hedera · IVY

9425 Helix. English Ivy. H 20. Handsome climber or ground-cover; excellent on north walls and under shrubs. Needs protection from the winter sun. 2½-in. pots, 1 to 9, 50c each; 10 to 29, 45c each; 30 to 100, 40c each. 4-in. pots, 1 to 9, 75c each; 10 to 29, 65c each.

9426 Helix baltica. Baltica Ivy. The hardiest of the Ivies. A small-leaved variety that is excellent for north and west exposures. 2½-in. pots, 1 to 9, 50c each; 10 to 29, 45c each; 30 to 100, 40c each. 4-in. pots, 1 to 9, 75c each; 10 to 29, 65c each.

Polygonum Auberti SILVER LACE-VINE

9436 H 40. Rapid grower. Blooms in late summer. 2-yr., 90c each.

WISTERIA

9438 Sinensis. The old favorite lavender-blue variety. 2-yr., 90c each.

9430
HONEYSUCKLE, GOLDFLAME

SHIPPING WEIGHTS FOR VINES. In 2½-in. pots, one plant weighs 1 lb.; add ½ lb. for each additional. In 4-in. pots, one weighs 3 lbs.; add 2 lbs. for each additional. In gal. cans, each 12 lbs. Vines not in containers, one weighs 2½ lbs.; add 1 lb. for each additional.

9436 **SILVER LACE-VINE (Polygonum Auberti)**

9438 **WISTERIA SINENSIS**

PORTER-WALTON COMPANY

SEED GRAIN

OATS

2534 Bannock. A highly smut-resistant variety that is a high yielder. Large, plump, white kernels. The straw is stiff and slightly shorter than other varieties.

2538 New Overland. (Certified.) Prodigious yielder of large, plump, white grains borne on short, stiff straws, always erect, seldom lodges, free from smut and rust.

2530 Swedish Select. The grain is plump, white, and very heavy. The quality of the Oats produced in the Rocky Mountains is unsurpassed.

BARLEY

2522 Trebi (Certified). An excellent feed variety and heavy yielder, recommended for the lands of the Rocky Mountain area. Where grown under irrigation, it qualifies as a malt Barley.

2524 Velvon (Certified). Highly resistant to covered smut and has a smooth awn, which greatly increases its value as feed. Large, plump, white kernels.

SPRING WHEAT

2552 Federation. A short, fairly early Spring Wheat. The kernels are white, rather short, and usually soft. It has replaced almost all other spring varieties.

2554 Lemhi. A variety that is rapidly replacing Dicklow. Its superiority is due to the fact that it has the milling quality of Dicklow combined with the stiff straw and high yielding ability of Federation. Lemhi will not lodge or shatter as easily as other Spring Wheats.

FIELD SEED PRICES

Prices on all field seeds are quoted on page 57. Since the market changes rapidly on Field Seeds, the prices quoted herein are subject to change without notice. All quotations are f.o.b. Salt Lake City, Utah.

HYBRID FIELD CORN

Sow in drills 3 feet apart, using approximately 15 pounds of seed per acre.

2502 PORT-WALCO HYBRID No. 100

The New Leader

Without a peer in a medium-maturing hybrid for the particular farmer. Since its introduction growers in most areas have reported heaviest tonnage per acre in both green fodder and dry weight with Port-Walco Hybrid 100. Maturity 5 to 7 days earlier than U. S. 52, allowing a wider range of planting. It is a prodigious yielder of good solid ears that are long and thick, with very little taper. A strong and vigorous grower, producing tall, succulent stalks. Then too, the ears are set at a good height so there is little or no stalk breakage.

2504 U.S. HYBRID No. 52

Matures in about 110 days. Plants are very tall and lodge-resistant. Ears are large, smooth, somewhat tapering, with 16 to 18 rows of medium-depth grain. Adapted over a wide area and an excellent yielder. On good soils, it is a general all-purpose hybrid.

2505 PORT-WALCO HYBRID No. 90

The newly proved leader in the 90-day maturity class. The dark green plants of this high-yielding early hybrid retain their rich color even after the ears are well matured. This condition makes possible a feed of greater nutritive value. The ears are medium size and thick, with deep kernels.

2507 PORT-WALCO HYBRID No. 120

The outstanding silage variety, maturing in 110 to 120 days. Not only is it the heaviest fodder producer in our hybrid list, but it yields an equally good grain crop. Its short shanks permit easy harvesting and handling for silage purposes. The plants of No. 120 are rich dark green, retaining their color until after the ears are well matured. As silage, it possesses both higher food value and higher palatability.

STANDARD OPEN-POLLINATED CORNS

2512 MINNESOTA No. 13

The leading all-round, open-pollinated variety. A 90-day dent Corn, acclimated to this area. It is the heaviest producer of the medium-early varieties. Plants grow 7 to 8 feet tall, bearing ears 9 to 10 inches long. Makes splendid ensilage.

2520 IMPROVED LEAMING

Matures in 100 to 110 days. It will grow more tonnage to the acre than any other open-pollinated variety we know. Very heavy foliage, making it especially good for silage purposes. The ears and kernels are a little larger than Minnesota 13. Produces good yields of grain.

2512 CORN, Minnesota No. 13

SEED AND NURSERY SPECIALISTS

53

BETTER PASTURES FEED MORE CATTLE

NEW PASTURE MIXTURES

Formulated for HIGHER PALATABILITY
MAINTAINED PRODUCTIVITY
WIDE SOIL ADAPTABILITY

2670 **Mixture A.** For well-drained irrigated land, or damp fertile soil.

Ladino	1 lb.
Red Clover	3 lbs.
Alfalfa	3 lbs.
Tall Meadow Oat	4 lbs.
Orchard Grass	5 lbs.
Smooth Brome	5 lbs.
Total per acre	21 lbs.

2676 **Mixture B.** For alkaline and wet soils.

Strawberry clover	3 lbs.
Sweet Yellow clover	3 lbs.
Reed Canary grass	2 lbs.
Alta Fescue	6 lbs.
Smooth Brome	6 lbs.
Total per acre	20 lbs.

OTHER HAY AND COVER CROPS

FIELD PEAS

2880 **Canadian Field.** They enrich the soil and are splendid stock feed. For hay, they should be cut while the milk is in the vine forming the pod. Plant early in the spring at the rate of 100 to 120 pounds per acre or 60 pounds with a nurse crop of Oats or Spring Rye.

SOY BEANS

2911 **Chief.** Outstanding for all purposes—hay, feed, hogging down, as well as for planting with corn for the silo. 100 days.

VETCH

2940 **Common.** Grown as a hay and seed crop, as well as for green manure, silage, and pasturage. Sow 60 to 80 pounds per acre.

SMALL GRAINS AND FORAGE CROPS

MILLET

2890 **Early Fortune or Red Hog.** Compact heads of shiny, reddish brown seeds. 50 to 60 days.
2892 **Golden or German.** This is one of the best varieties for hay and fodder, yielding 3 to 5 tons of hay per acre.
2894 **Yellow Hog.** Mainly a grain crop but the hay is of a good quality for feeding purposes.

SUNFLOWER

2930 **Grey Stripe.** A good silage crop for dry land. Very palatable and has high food value. Plant 5 to 6 pounds per acre.

DRY-LAND GRAIN SORGHUMS

2920 **60-Day Milo** (Dwarf or Combine Strain). Similar to Kaffir Corn but shorter. Grows erect, with thick, close-jointed stalks 2 to 3 feet tall. The large heads give a heavy yield of grain. It is drought-resistant and does well on alkaline soils.

SWEET SORGHUMS

2924 **Atlas Sorgo.** Extremely drought-resistant. Produces a long, leafy stalk, sweet and juicy, with a good grain head.
2928 **Black Amber Cane.** 80 to 100 days. The best-known Sorgo and in many sections the favorite because it is the earliest.

KOCHIA

2916 **Scoparia.** This is the most productive variety, growing 4 to 5 feet tall and yielding 5 to 7 tons of hay per acre when under irrigation. On alkaline soil it yields equally well. The hay contains 4 to 8 per cent more protein than alfalfa.

Kochia is one of the most drought resistant forage plants available for dry land planting. Sow seed at the rate of 6 pounds per acre on irrigated land or 3 pounds per acre on dry land in late fall or early spring.

RAPE

2900 **Dwarf Essex.** Fall, winter or spring pasture for hogs, sheep, and poultry. Sow 10 pounds per acre.

ABOUT PRICES

All field seed prices are quoted on page 57.

The prices quoted herein are subject to market changes. You are safe, however, in sending remittance according to these prices. In case of decline, the difference will be promptly refunded; if there has been an advance, you will be notified for your confirmation before shipment is made.

8981 MULTIFLORA ROSE

A Permanent Low-Cost Fence. Requires No Maintenance

Fast Growing. Makes a dense, stock-tight fence in three to five years.

Eliminates Fence Line Weeds.

Does Not Spread. Multiflora Roses do not sucker.

Requires No Maintenance. Eliminates fence repairing costs. Needs no clipping, pruning or training. Just irrigate during the first year to get the new plants established, and keep the weeds down for two years.

Set plants 18 inches apart in fall or early spring.

Prices per plant F.O.B. Salt Lake City

100 to 225	$0 07
250 to 975	06
1000 to 9975	05
10,000 up	04½

Shipping weight approximately 50 lbs. per 1000.

ASK FOR P.-W.'s FREE BULLETIN ON FARM AND FORAGE SEEDS. This contains authentic, dependable information on the value and adaptability of the various Farm and Range Clovers and Grasses, together with planting and cultural directions.

CLOVER FOR MEADOWS AND PASTURES

2600 Alsike. Recommended both for sowing with timothy and also with the Red and Mammoth Clovers, as well as a hay crop by itself. It does not winter-kill. The use of Alsike Clover is increasing rapidly; cattle prefer it to other Clovers and it is very fine for honey-bees. Sow at the rate of 6 or 8 pounds per acre; sown in mixtures, 5 or 6 pounds per acre is sufficient. **Does best on damp soils.** Used in pasture mixture with grasses.

2610 Hubam. The richest honey-producing Clover. An annual sweet Clover which grows rapidly, attaining a height of 6 to 7 feet. It is very valuable for pasturage and hay when cut before it gets too old. Also used to great advantage as a cover crop or for green manure. Sow 12 to 15 pounds per acre in fall or spring.

2620 Ladino. Regarded as a large form of the common White Dutch Clover and like the latter is a long-lived perennial. After being grazed, new leaves develop quickly and complete recovery occurs in 17 to 28 days. It is strictly a crop for irrigation. Sow in fall or spring at the rate of 7 to 8 pounds per acre.

2630 Medium Red (*Trifolium pratense*). A dependable, all-round variety for farmers and stockmen. It makes hay crops each year. Sow in either spring or fall at the rate of 15 pounds to the acre. It is good in pastures either alone or with some grass as a companion crop and is replacing alfalfa in heavily wilt-infested areas.

2640 Strawberry (Tall Variety). Similar to Ladino but has proved to be much hardier. The flower resembles White Dutch Clover, but is pink. The foliage is similar to White Clover, having creeping runners, strawberry fashion, establishing new plants wherever the nodes contact the soil. **It has proved particularly adaptable to alkaline and wet soils.** Much in demand as a pasture crop because of its palatability. Sow 4 to 6 pounds per acre.

2650 White Dutch. A long-lived perennial legume, spreading by creeping stems that root at the nodes. When grown in mixtures with grass it increases the carrying capacity of the pasture and provides a nutritious and palatable feed.

SWEET CLOVER

2660 White Blossom (*Melilotus alba*). Its value in the redemption of alkali lands cannot be overestimated. It grows in a variety of soils—heavy, light, wet or dry, almost anywhere except in acid soil. Sow 10 to 14 pounds per acre.

2666 Yellow Blossom (*Melilotus officinalis*). Finer in the stalk and more palatable when mature than White Blossom, and has the same soil adaptation. Its refinement of stalk and palatability make it a good pasture and hay crop.

ALFALFA (Lucerne) *Wonder Crop of the West*

2560 Hardy Desert. This splendid variety is the selection from the far-famed Utah Dry Land type, which is a "Northern Hardy" strain. It produces even under adverse conditions but in favorable situations under irrigation, it is a prodigious yielder. Sow 10 to 15 pounds per acre.

2570 Utah Pioneer (Certified). Selected from two parent fields in Millard County which are known to be at least 60 years old without reseeding or breaking up. Has exceptional resistance to wilt.

2580 Grimm. Especially recommended for shallow soils, those underlaid with hardpan, or where the watertable is near the surface. The stems and leaves are of somewhat finer and leafier quality than common Alfalfa. It is susceptible to bacterial wilt and is not recommended for areas of severe infestation.

2590 Ladak. Tests at nearly every northern and western Experiment Station show Ladak leading on tonnage, long life, drought-resistance, and winter hardiness. It has also shown marked resistance to bacterial wilt. Ladak makes an exceptionally heavy first and second crop but little third.

2578 Ranger. This new variety, which is highly resistant to bacterial wilt, was developed by the Nebraska Experiment Station in cooperation with the U.S.D.A. Being very similar to the common or Hardy Desert variety in habit of growth and soil requirements, it is well adapted to northern areas. In localities where bacterial wilt is a problem, a stand of Ranger will remain indefinitely.

See page 57 for prices.

GRASS for RANGE, MEADOW, PASTURE

2700 MOUNTAIN BROME GRASS
(Bromus marginatus)

This stout perennial bunch grass is very common in altitudes of 5000 to 10,000 feet. It has a very wide range of soil adaptation, varying from fairly moist loamy soils where the best growth is made, to fairly dry, gravelly soils. Mountain Brome Grass, when young, is grazed closely by all kinds of livestock. Where it can be cut for hay, it makes a very fine feed for horses and cattle.

It is an exceptional grass for the reclamation of land inaccessible to farm machinery, for good stands may be obtained by broadcasting on areas where seedbed preparation is not possible. Sow 10 to 20 pounds per acre.

2740 MEADOW FESCUE

The leaves are bright green and very succulent, supplying palatable forage from early spring until late fall. Sow 20 to 30 pounds per acre.

2710 SMOOTH BROME GRASS
(Bromus inermis)

Smooth Brome is one of the outstanding grasses for the Intermountain area, being well adapted to arid regions where rainfall is relatively low. It is the most palatable of all the important grasses, surpassing even the well-known Kentucky Blue Grass in this respect. Smooth Brome is a long-lived perennial with numerous creeping rootstalks that form a dense heavy sod, making it capable of standing much abuse as a pasture grass. Brome thrives especially well on a rich loamy soil; but in the wild state it grows in dry, gravelly soils, or even in pure sand. Recent experiments have shown it to succeed in alkaline soils.

The stems attain a height of 2 to 3 feet. Two cuttings of hay are generally obtained in a season, yields ranging from 1 to 4 tons per acre. Sow 10 to 20 pounds per acre. Drilling is preferable to broadcasting wherever possible.

For Field Seed Prices, see page 57

GRASS SEED, continued

SUDAN GRASS

2750 ORCHARD GRASS
(Dactylis glomerata)

This very early pasture grass furnishes feed at least three weeks before most other grasses. Even after close grazing, a ten-day interval is sufficient for another growth. It makes a heavy sod and gives splendid pasture until late in the fall. Withstands drought and is very hardy. It grows in tufts and can be sown, if desired, with red clover and alfalfa. When planted alone, sow at the rate of 20 to 25 pounds per acre.

2780 CRESTED WHEAT GRASS
(Agropyron cristatum)

This wonderful ranch and range grass grows earlier in the spring and later in the fall because of its ability to grow at low temperatures. As a hay crop it is very nutritious and palatable and stands well under grazing. It has made a most remarkable showing under arid conditions, succeeding where many other varieties fail. Crested Wheat is a long-lived grass. Fields twenty years old are still doing well. It is relished by livestock and adapts itself to a wide range of soils. Sow 10 pounds per acre.

2735 ALTA FESCUE
(Festuca elatior arundinacea)

Alta Fescue is one of the most outstanding grasses of recent development for both pasture and hay purposes. It is much more productive and palatable than Meadow Fescue. It grows late in the summer and fall when other grasses have passed their productive peak. Various trials show it to outyield other varieties from 15 to 50 per cent. The dense root system, reaching a depth of 5 to 6 feet, makes this variety valuable as a soil builder where the humus content is low. It also crowds out undesirable weed growth. Sow 12 to 15 pounds per acre.

2760 PERENNIAL RYE GRASS

A desirable grass for pastures, its chief value being as an ingredient in permanent pasture mixtures. Sow 20 to 25 pounds per acre.

2810 SLENDER WHEAT GRASS

This is a native North American bunch grass, which has proved very valuable under cultivation. It is a bunch-forming variety, being better adapted to range land than meadows; however, recent tests are proving its value as a grass for alkaline soils. It is recommended for pastures in canyons or flats, succeeding exceptionally well at high elevations. It grows in arid sections, producing numerous slender, erect stems 2 to 4 feet high, with narrow flat leaves.

2820 WESTERN WHEAT GRASS
(Agropyron Smithi)

A variety of great promise for arid western regions. It is erect in growth and forms a firm solid turf even where moisture is very limited. It produces a uniform turf, which makes it most suitable for fairways, roadside planting, and erosion control as well as an excellent range grass where rainfall is light.

2830 RED TOP

A valuable grass for moist and alkaline soils. Sow 15 to 25 pounds per acre.

2840 REED CANARY GRASS
(Phalaris arundinacea)

This is a valuable, high-yielding forage plant that is naturally adapted to low wet lands as a permanent source of high-quality hay and good pasturage. Two or three crops of hay and some fall pasture may be obtained. Sow it at the rate of 5 to 6 pounds per acre broadcast or in drills, or 2 to 3 pounds per acre in 16 to 18-inch rows.

2934 SUDAN GRASS (Common)

Drill 15 to 20 pounds or broadcast 25 pounds per acre for pasture. It will endure much alkali. Planted in rich soil in June, it will be ready to pasture in 30 days, furnishing grazing for two cows per acre throughout the summer. As a hay crop, it should be cut when heads appear. Allow several days of ideal weather to cure. A second crop may be cut or pastured, as preferred.

2935 NEW SWEET SUDAN GRASS

This new variety is a development resulting from several years' breeding work by the Texas Agricultural Experiment Station in cooperation with the Bureau of Plant Industry, U. S. Department of Agriculture. It is sweet, juicy and more palatable to livestock than Common Sudan, thereby producing more vegetative growth and remaining green longer than the Common. After the crop reaches maturity the stalks and stems are still eaten readily. Sweet Sudan has more and broader leaves, heavier and taller stalks, and stools much heavier than Common Sudan.

2850 TALL MEADOW OAT GRASS

Tall Meadow Oat is a long-lived, deep-rooted and drought-resistant perennial grass. It produces an abundance of very palatable forage from early spring until late fall. Recent pasture experiments conducted by U.S.A.C. at Logan prove this grass to be one of the most desirable from the standpoint of productivity and palatability, comparing very favorably with Smooth Brome. Tall Meadow Oat Grass gives best results for pasture when sown in a mixture with other grasses and clover.

2860 TIMOTHY

Of hay grasses, Timothy leads all. Thrives on clay or heavy loams, wet or boggy soils, or in mountainous districts. At higher elevations where fewer grasses and clovers are adaptable, Timothy is the most important hay and pasture crop. Alone, sow 12 pounds to the acre, or with clover, 10 pounds Timothy and 6 pounds clover.

About Prices

From time to time we will be sending our customers special FIELD SEED LISTS to correct changes in market prices. If you are not receiving them please inform

FIELD SEED PRICES

TANT: All field seed prices are subject to market changes. You are safe, however, in sending remittance based on ices. In case of decline, the difference will be promptly refunded; when an advance has been necessary, you will be for your confirmation before shipment is made.

For 5 to 9 pounds add 1c per pound to the 10-pound rate.
For 1 to 4 pounds add 3c per pound to the 10-pound rate.

FIELD CORN HYBRIDS
See page 53

	5 to 9 lbs. per lb.	10 to 55 lbs. per lb.	1 to 9 bu. per bu.	10 bu. up per bu.
rt-Walco No. 90	$0 19	$0 18	$9 50	$9 25
rt-Walco No. 00	19	18	9 50	9 25
rt-Walco No. 20	19	18	9 50	9 25

IELD CORN (Open-Pollinated)
See page 53

	10 to 24 lbs. per lb.	25 to 99 lbs. per lb.	1 to 9 bags per cwt.	10 bags per cwt.
innesota 13	$0 11½	$0 10½	$9 40	$9 25
proved Leaming	11½	10½	9 40	9 25

SS SEEDS—Pasture and Dry Land
See pages 55 and 56

	10 to 24 lbs. per lb.	25 to 99 lbs. per lb.	Bag lots per 100 lbs.
ome Grass (Smooth)	$0 58	$0 57	$56 00
ountain Brome Grass	36½	35½	34 50
eadow Fescue, Fancy	44½	43½	42 50
ta Fescue, Blue Tag	80	79	78 00
chard Grass, Fancy	44½	43½	42 50
ed Canary Grass		Ask	
d Top, 92% Pure	76½	75½	74 50
e Grass, Perennial,			
lue Tag	25½	24½	23 50
ender Wheat Grass	41	40	39 00
estern Wheat Grass	48	47	46 00
dan Grass, Fancy	15½	14½	13 50
ew Sweet Sudan Grass	17½	16½	15 50
ll Meadow Oat Grass	69	68	67 00
mothy, 99.50% Pure	41	40	39 00
ested Wheat Grass	44½	43½	42 50

ALFALFA SEED
See page 55

	10 to 24 lbs. per lb.	25 to 99 lbs. per lb.	Bag lots per 100 lbs.
tah Hardy Desert, Ex- ra Fancy	$0 55½	$0 54½	$53 50
tah Hardy Desert, Fancy	53½	52½	51 50
rimm, Blue Tag	67	66	65 00
dak, Blue Tag	74	73	72 00
tah Pioneer, Blue Tag	60	59	58 00
anger, Certified	92	91	90 00
uth African	42	41	40 00

CLOVERS
See page 55

	10 to 24 lbs. per lb.	25 to 99 lbs. per lb.	Bag lots per 100 lbs.
lsike, 99% Pure	$0 47	$0 46	$45 00
ubam, Annual	31	30	29 00
dino Certified	2 02	2 01	200 00
dino Uncertified	1 92	1 91	190 00
ed Clover, Medium	59	58	57 00
trawberry	1 14	1 13	112 00
weet White Blossom, Premium Grade	26½	25½	24 50
weet Yellow Blossom	25½	24½	23 50
hite Dutch Clover 99% Pure	1 13	1 12	111 00
hite Dutch with 9% Alsike	94	93	92 00

P.-W.'s PASTURE MIXTURES
See page 54

		10 to 24 lbs. per lb.	25 to 99 lbs. per lb.	Bag lots per 100 lbs.
2670	(A) For Well-Drained Irrigated Land or Damp Fertile Soils	$0 64	$0 63	$62 00
2676	(B) For Alkaline and Wet Soils	73½	72½	71 50

GRAINS (Seed Stock)
See page 53

		Bag lots per 100 lbs.	Ton lots per 100 lbs.
2522	Barley, Trebi, Certified	$5 00	$4 90
2524	Barley, Velvon, Certified	5 00	4 90
2530	Oats, Swedish Select, Certified	5 50	5 40
2534	Oats, Bannock, Certified	5 50	5 40
2538	Oats, Overland	5 50	5 40
2552	Wheat, Federation, Certified	5 75	5 65
2554	Wheat, Lemhi, Certified	5 75	5 65

OTHER FARM SEED
See page 54

		10 to 24 lbs. per lb.	25 to 99 lbs. per lb.	Bag lots per cwt.
2880	Canadian Field Peas, Extra Fancy	$0 12	$0 11	$10 00
2890	Millet, Early Fortune	10	09	8 00
2892	Millet, Golden or German	14½	13½	12 75
2894	Millet, Yellow Hog, Large Millet	10	09	8 00
2920	Milo Maize, 60-Day	11½	10½	9 50
2900	Rape, Dwarf Essex	20	19	18 00
2928	Sorghum, Black Amber Cane	13	12	11 00
2924	Sorgo, Atlas	12	11	10 00
2911	Soy Beans, Chief	14	13	12 25
2930	Sunflower, Grey Stripe	25½	24½	23 50
2940	Vetch, Common or Spring	18	17	16 00
2916	Kochia scoparia			$1.15 per lb.

MANGELS

		1 to 4 lbs. per lb.	5 to 24 lbs. per lb.	25 to 99 lbs. per lb.	100 lbs. per lb.
87	Giant Half Sugar Rose	$0 65	$0 55	$0 53	$0 50
89	Giant Sludstrup	65	55	53	50

CARROTS (for Stock Feed)

		1 to 4 lbs. per lb.	5 to 24 lbs. per lb.
132	Improved Long Orange	$1 80	$1 60
134	Mastodon or Short White	1 80	1 60

NOTICE

Field seed prices are quoted subject to market fluctuations which result in frequent changes.

If your remittance is more than the market price the difference will be refunded.

In case of an advance your confirmation will be solicited before shipment is made.

AND NURSERY SPECIALISTS

9900 BLACKBERRY, Early Harvest

BLACKBERRIES

9900 **Early Harvest.** Berries uniform, glossy black. Very early.
9906 **Lucretia Dewberry.** Fruit very large; superb quality.

All Blackberries, 1 to 9, 15c each; 10 to 29, 12c each; 30 to 249, 10c each; 250 to 1000, 9c each

BOYSENBERRIES

9912 **Thornless.** Superior to all other vine berries in flavor, color, size and productiveness. 2-yr. transplants. 1 to 9, 40c each; 10 to 29, 35c each; 30 to 249, 28c each; 250 to 1000, 25c each.

CURRANTS

9920 **Perfection.** Large, bright red. The most popular new variety. Large 2-yr. roots. 1 to 9, 50c each; 10 to 29, 40c each; 30 to 249, 34c each.

BLACK AND PURPLE RASPBERRIES

9980 **Bristol** (Black). The berries are large, firm, fairly glossy and of excellent quality.
9984 **Sodus** (Purple). Vigorous and very productive. Hardy, drought-resistant plants that yield a good crop every year. The fruits are large, firm, medium purple in color.

Each of above, 1 to 9, 23c each; 10 to 49, 18c each; 50 to 249, 12c each; 250 to 1000, 10c each

RED RASPBERRIES

9970 **Latham.** This very desirable variety is certified mosaic-free. Berries are large and round, with profitable shipping firmness and brilliant red color. 10 to 49, 12c each; 50 to 249, 10c each; 250 to 1000, 8c each.
9974 **P.-W.'s Colossus Everbearing.** The fruits are very large, firm, and of excellent flavor and color. Fine for freezing. Bears in spring and fall.
9976 **Indian Summer.** Another everbearing Raspberry of superior quality. The fruits are large, medium red and of top flavor. The vigorous plants bear heavy crops—the first soon after the June varieties and the second from September until frost.

All Red Raspberries except Latham, 1 to 9, 23c each; 10 to 49, 18c each; 50 to 249, 12c each; 250 to 1000, 10c each

58

GOOSEBERRIES

9930 **Champion.** Medium-sized red fruits. A good yielder. 1 to 9, 60c each; 10 to 29, 50c each; 30 to 249, 45c each; 250 to 1000, 40c each.
9936 **Poorman.** A splendid Gooseberry with large red fruits of highest quality. 1 to 9, $1.00 each; 10 to 29, 90c each; 30 to 249, 80c each; 250 to 1000, 70c each.

GRAPES, Hardy American

9940 **Caco.** Hardy red Grape. Large, juicy and delicious. 1 to 9, 45c each; 10 to 29, 37c each; 30 to 249, 33c each; 250 to 1000, 30c each.
9942 **Concord.** Deep purple. Most popular for jelly or grape juice. 1 to 9, 35c each; 10 to 29, 30c each; 30 to 249, 25c each; 250 to 1000, 22c each.
9948 **Golden Muscat.** Very large clusters and berries. The fruit is tender, sweet, juicy and aromatic. Ripens 10 days later than Concord.
9950 **Keuka.** Medium-sized berries, dark red with a heavy overcast which gives them a lilac color. The flesh is juicy and sweet, with very tender skin. September.
9953 **Portland.** This new early white Grape has risen to first place in its class. Vigorous and productive. 1 to 9, 45c each; 10 to 29, 37c each; 30 to 249, 33c each; 250 to 1000, 30c each.
9956 **Seneca.** A green California-type Grape on a hardy vine. The firm, meaty flesh of superlative quality keeps well either on the vine or off. Ripens 3 weeks before Concord.
9958 **Van Buren.** Ripens a month earlier than Concord. The fruit is of the Concord type and equal to it in quality.

Any of above, except where noted, 1 to 9, $1.00 each; 10 to 29, 90c each

GRAPES, European

9960 **Black Malvoisie.** Berries large, oblong, reddish black, juicy.
9962 **Flame Tokay.** Large, sweet, red.
9964 **Muscat.** Large, light-colored raisin and wine Grape.
9966 **Thompson Seedless.** Popular table Grape.

All European Grapes, 1 to 9, 45c each; 10 to 29, 37c each; 30 to 249, 33c each

All Grape-vines are 2-yr. No. 1 plants

STRAWBERRIES

All Strawberry plants will be sent by either Parcel Post or Express, according to quantity. They are packed in bunches of 25 plants each.

9990 **Marshall.** The best main-crop variety. The color is a rich, glistening crimson.
9992 **Mastodon Everbearing.** Large, luscious, deep red.
9997 **Utah Centennial.** The finest new everbearing Strawberry of the century. The giant, dark red berries have a distinctive flavor combining piquancy with sweetness. Amazingly productive. The fruits handle very well in marketing.

Strawberries are sold only in bunches of approximately 25 plants each.

	25 to 50 each	75 to 225 each	250 to 975 each	1000 up each
Marshall	$0 04	$0 03	$0 02½	$0 02
Mastodon	05	04	03	02½
Utah Centennial	08	06	05	04

9912 BOYSENBERRY, Thornless

PORTER-WALTON COMPANY

P.-W.'s FRUIT TREES
Mountain Grown for Greater Productivity

SWEET CHERRIES

Plant 30 feet apart; 49 per acre.

9800 **Bing.** About one week earlier than Lambert. One of the best market Cherries. Large, dark red, nearly black. Meat firm, sweet, and exceedingly well flavored. Ripens in July in Salt Lake valley. A wonderful shipper. $\frac{7}{16}-\frac{9}{16}$, $\frac{9}{16}-\frac{11}{16}$, $\frac{11}{16}$–up.

9802 **Lambert.** Follows Bing in ripening and is fully equal to it as a commercial and home variety. Fruit very large, heart-shaped; firm flesh of rich, sweet flavor. It is less subject to frost injury in blossom time than any other sweet variety. Ripens in July. $\frac{7}{16}-\frac{9}{16}$, $\frac{9}{16}-\frac{11}{16}$, $\frac{11}{16}$–up.

9804 **Black Tartarian.** Large, purplish black, sweet. Ripens first of July. *Plant with Bing or Lambert for Pollination.* $\frac{7}{16}-\frac{9}{16}$, $\frac{9}{16}-\frac{11}{16}$.

9806 **Napoleon.** Very large, pale yellow with red cheek. June. $\frac{7}{16}-\frac{9}{16}$, $\frac{9}{16}-\frac{11}{16}$–up.

Sour Cherries

Plant 20 feet apart each way; 108 per acre.

9812 **Montmorency Improved.** This strain produces much larger fruit than the old true Montmorency and has become the leading sour Cherry for cold pack and canning. Ripens late June to early July. $\frac{7}{16}-\frac{9}{16}$, $\frac{9}{16}-\frac{3}{4}$.

Hansen's Bush Cherries

9214 Hardy, easy to grow, and early bearing, they adapt themselves to even the coldest climates. The fruit is good to eat fresh and makes delicious preserves. When used as ornamental shrubs they are beautiful as specimens, groups or hedges. 2 to 3 ft., 1 to 9, 90c each; 10 to 29, 80c each; 30 to 100, 75c each.

DWARF FRUIT TREES

Only a small space is required for these fruitful and ornamental Dwarf Trees. Even a small yard can provide a wide variety of delicious fruit. Usually these trees begin bearing the first or second year after planting and are the most efficient way to use garden space.

Popular demand for Dwarf Fruit Trees has guided us in the selection of this group of fine varieties, the largest we have ever offered. There is a fruit for every month from June to October.

9793 **Dwarf Apricot, Moorpark.** (June.)
9799 **Dwarf Cherry, Bing.** (July.)
9835 **Dwarf Peach, Hale Haven.** (August.)
9869 **Dwarf Pear, Bartlett.** (September.)
9899 **Dwarf Prune, Italian.** (September.)
9868 **Dwarf Apple, Red Delicious.** (October.)
Husky, 2-year-old trees, $3.00 each.
f.o.b. Salt Lake City
Shipping weights: 1 tree 4½ lbs.; each additional tree 1½ lbs.

SHIPPING WEIGHTS

Size	One Tree	Each Additional Tree
$\frac{5}{16}-\frac{7}{16}$	3½ lbs.	1 lb.
$\frac{7}{16}-\frac{9}{16}$	4½ lbs.	1½ lbs.
$\frac{9}{16}-\frac{11}{16}$	6½ lbs.	2 lbs.
$\frac{11}{16}$–up	9 lbs.	5 lbs.

SEED AND NURSERY SPECIALISTS

PEACHES

Plant 20 to 25 feet apart each way; 70 to 108 per acre.

9820 **Alexander.** Handsome crimson fruit. Ripens about July 24.

9828 **Early Elberta.** About ten days earlier than regular Elberta. Has sweeter flesh.

9826 **Elberta.** A leading market variety. Large, handsome, bright yellow overspread with crimson; juicy. Fine shipper. Freestone.

8933 **Halberta.** A beautiful red-checked giant Peach with solid yellow flesh of delicious flavor. Very hardy and productive, ripening about five days later than J. H. Hale.

9836 **Hale Haven.** Large, reddish yellow. A cross between J. H. Hale and South Haven, combining the good qualities of both. Ripens 17 days before Elberta.

9834 **J. H. Hale.** Large, orange-yellow. Considered by many to be superior to Elberta. Freestone.

9840 **Orange Cling.** Very large. Yellow with dark crimson cheek; flesh golden yellow.

9831 **Summer Elberta.** A new, superior, very early, yellow-fleshed freestone Peach. Sweet, juicy flesh and beautiful red skin. Excellent for canning, shipping and for eating fresh. Ripens in July and early August.

Sizes of Peaches: $\frac{5}{16}-\frac{7}{16}$, $\frac{7}{16}-\frac{9}{16}$, $\frac{9}{16}-\frac{11}{16}$, $\frac{11}{16}$–up.

Price Schedules on Cherries and Peaches

See each variety for sizes available	Prices per tree for quantities of one variety and size			
CHERRIES	1 to 9 trees	10 to 49 trees	50 to 249 trees	250–up trees
$\frac{7}{16}-\frac{9}{16}$ (4 ft.)	$1.25	$1.05	$0.90	
$\frac{9}{16}-\frac{11}{16}$ (5 ft.)	1.50	1.20	1.00	
$\frac{11}{16}$–up (6 ft.)	1.75	1.40	1.25	
PEACHES				
$\frac{5}{16}-\frac{7}{16}$ (3 ft.)	.75	.60	.50	$0.45
$\frac{7}{16}-\frac{9}{16}$ (4 ft.)	1.00	.75	.60	.55
$\frac{9}{16}-\frac{11}{16}$ (5 ft.)	1.25	.90	.70	.65
$\frac{11}{16}$–up (6 ft.)	1.50	1.00	.80	.75

f.o.b. Salt Lake City

Dwarf Fruit Tree Orchard

P.-W.'S FRUIT TREES, continued

APPLES

Plant 35 feet apart each way; 36 per acre.

Summer Varieties

9750 Early Redbird. Claimed to be the earliest red Apple in cultivation. Ripens a week earlier than Yellow Transparent. Because of its large size, excellent flavor and cooking qualities, it is superseding the old favorite, Red Astrachan.

9757 Summer Delicious. Similar to Red Delicious in size, shape, color and flavor, but it ripens in July and August. An exceptional home orchard or early market Apple.

9756 Yellow Transparent. One of the earliest. Pale yellow when ripe; good quality. Ripens in July.

Sizes of Summer Apples: ⁵⁄₁₆–⁷⁄₁₆, ⁷⁄₁₆–⁹⁄₁₆, ⁹⁄₁₆–¹¹⁄₁₆.

Autumn Varieties

9746 Wealthy. Dark red, sub-acid. Trees bear very young.

Sizes: ⁵⁄₁₆–⁷⁄₁₆, ⁷⁄₁₆–⁹⁄₁₆, ⁹⁄₁₆–¹¹⁄₁₆.

Winter Varieties

9762 Delicious. Solid red. Most popular for eating, storing and shipping.

9764 Delicious, Yellow-gold. It bears young and heavily. The fruit is large and juicy. No other yellow Apple is of better quality.

9766 Jonathan. Solid red. Equal to Delicious in popularity. Very firm, richly flavored flesh.

9772 Rome Beauty. Solid red. A brilliant red Apple, large, tender, juicy. The tree is hardy and bears heavy crops every year.

9774 Stayman's Winesap. Smooth, greenish yellow, splashed and striped with red and purple.

Sizes of Winter Apples: ⁵⁄₁₆–⁷⁄₁₆, ⁷⁄₁₆–⁹⁄₁₆, ⁹⁄₁₆–¹¹⁄₁₆.

SHIPPING WEIGHTS

Size	One Tree	Each Additional Tree
⁵⁄₁₆–⁷⁄₁₆	3½ lbs.	1 lb.
⁷⁄₁₆–⁹⁄₁₆	4½ lbs.	1½ lbs.
⁹⁄₁₆–¹¹⁄₁₆	6½ lbs.	2 lbs.
¹¹⁄₁₆–up	9 lbs.	5 lbs.

9762 APPLE, Delicious

Crab Apples

9787 Strawberry. Bright crimson, conical-shaped fruits of exceptional quality. For jelly, preserves or pies it is superior to Siberian Crab and is sweet enough to be eaten fresh. Sizes: ⁵⁄₁₆–⁷⁄₁₆, ⁷⁄₁₆–⁹⁄₁₆, ⁹⁄₁₆–¹¹⁄₁₆.

NECTARINES

The Nectarine has a smooth skin like a plum. Its juicy green flesh has a fresh, distinctive flavor. Set trees 16 to 18 feet apart.

9816 John Rivers. The hardiest Nectarine. Attractive size, red cheek and luscious green flesh.

Sizes: ⁷⁄₁₆–⁹⁄₁₆, ⁹⁄₁₆–¹¹⁄₁₆, ¹¹⁄₁₆–up.

PLUMS and PRUNES

Plant about 20 feet apart each way; 108 per acre

9873 Elephant Heart. Early Strain. A huge, heart-shaped, freestone Plum with blood-red flesh and luscious flavor. Early September.

9872 Formosa. Early, large, heart-shaped, cherry-red as it ripens, sweet and delicious. Early July.

9874 Green Gage. Large, pale green fruits, rich flavored and juicy.

9886 Santa Rosa. One of the leading shippers. Purplish red fruit of good size. Flesh reddish in color, juicy and delicious. Late July.

9890 Satsuma. A fine, large purplish crimson Plum; pit small. Delicious flavor. July.

9898 ITALIAN FELLENBERG PRUNE. Large, oval, dark purple. Flesh greenish yellow, separating freely from stone; best for drying. August, September. Best commercial sort; on peach root. Sizes: ⁵⁄₁₆–⁷⁄₁₆, ⁷⁄₁₆–⁹⁄₁₆; ⁹⁄₁₆–¹¹⁄₁₆, ¹¹⁄₁₆–up.

APPLES, APRICOTS, PEARS, PLUMS AND NECTARINES 2-yr. trees

Prices per tree for quantities of one variety and size

See each fruit for sizes available

Sizes		1 to 9 trees	10 to 49 trees	50 to 249 trees	250 or more trees
⁵⁄₁₆–⁷⁄₁₆	(3 ft.)	$0.75	$0.60	$0.50	$0.45
⁷⁄₁₆–⁹⁄₁₆	(4 ft.)	1.00	.75	.60	.55
⁹⁄₁₆–¹¹⁄₁₆	(5 ft.)	1.25	.90	.70	.65
¹¹⁄₁₆–up	(6 ft.)	1.50	1.00	.80	.75

f.o.b. Salt Lake City

"3 on 1" APPLE TREE

Cat. No. 9739

Grow 3 different kinds of Apples on one tree.

On one of these three-variety-combination Apple trees you get as many kinds as are usually grown in the average home orchard. **Yellow Transparent** (an excellent early summer Apple for eating or sauce), **Jonathan** (richly flavored fall and winter Apple) and **Red Rome Beauty** (highly acclaimed for its quality as a fresh fruit and for baking or pies). All grow on one tree.

"Three on One" Apple trees give you a long season of valuable fruit and help eliminate troublesome surpluses.

4 to 5-ft. trees, $3.00 each.

9790 **APRICOTS, Chinese**

P.-W s *Fruit Trees*

"Mountain Grown" for Greater Productivity

9873 **PLUMS, Elephant Heart.** See page 60

9898 **ITALIAN FELLENBERG PRUNES.** See page 60

APRICOTS

Plant about 25 feet apart each way

9790 **Chinese.** Large, round, deep orange-colored fruits. Because this Apricot retains its firmness when shipped, it is the leader for commercial orchard planting. Extra rich flavor and color, together with its sweet nut-like pit, are qualities desired by the majority for home use. Chinese Apricot is very productive, usually beginning to bear the third year after planting. Ripens late June. Sizes: 5/16–7/16, 7/16–9/16, 9/16–11/16, 11/16–up.

9796 **Moorpark.** Very large, light yellow, oval-shaped fruit. The tree is slightly hardier than Chinese. Late June.
Sizes: 7/16–9/16, 9/16–11/16.

See page 60 for prices

9764 **APPLE, Delicious Yellow-Gold**
See page 60

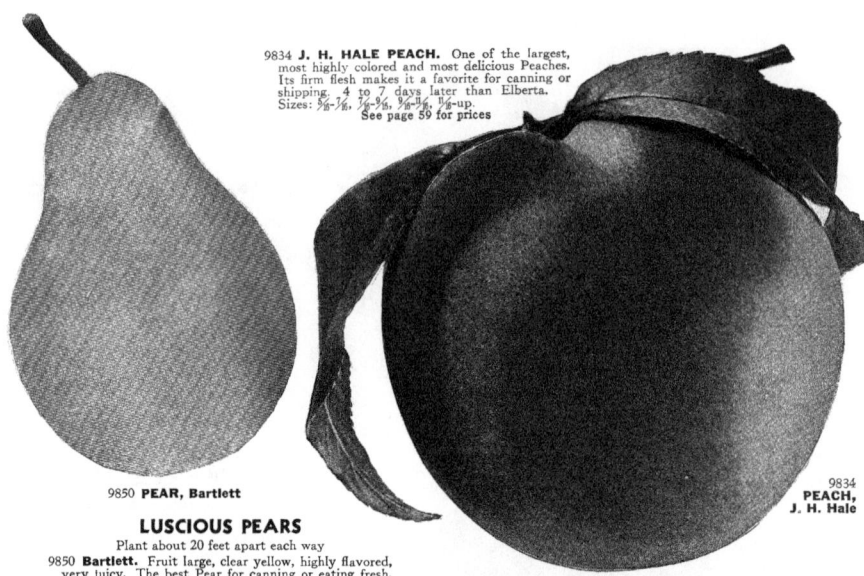

9834 **J. H. HALE PEACH.** One of the largest, most highly colored and most delicious Peaches. Its firm flesh makes it a favorite for canning or shipping. 4 to 7 days later than Elberta. Sizes: ⁵⁄₈–⁷⁄₈, ⁷⁄₈–⁹⁄₈, ⁹⁄₈–¹¹⁄₈, ¹¹⁄₈–up.
See page 59 for prices

9850 **PEAR, Bartlett**

9834
**PEACH,
J. H. Hale**

LUSCIOUS PEARS
Plant about 20 feet apart each way

9850 **Bartlett.** Fruit large, clear yellow, highly flavored, very juicy. The best Pear for canning or eating fresh. September.

9860 **Parrish Favorite.** Large winter Pear, ripening in November and December. Will keep until spring, retaining its captivating flavor. Never blights.

Sizes of Pears: ⁵⁄₁₆–⁷⁄₁₆, ⁷⁄₁₆–⁹⁄₁₆, ⁹⁄₁₆–¹¹⁄₁₆, ¹¹⁄₁₆–up.
See page 60 for prices

9831 **SUMMER ELBERTA PEACH.** A very early, yellow-fleshed, freestone Peach with sweet, juicy flesh and beautiful red skin. Excellent for canning, shipping and eating fresh. Ripens in July and early August.
Sizes: ⁵⁄₈–⁷⁄₈, ⁷⁄₈–⁹⁄₈, ⁹⁄₈–¹¹⁄₈, ¹¹⁄₈–up.
See page 59 for prices

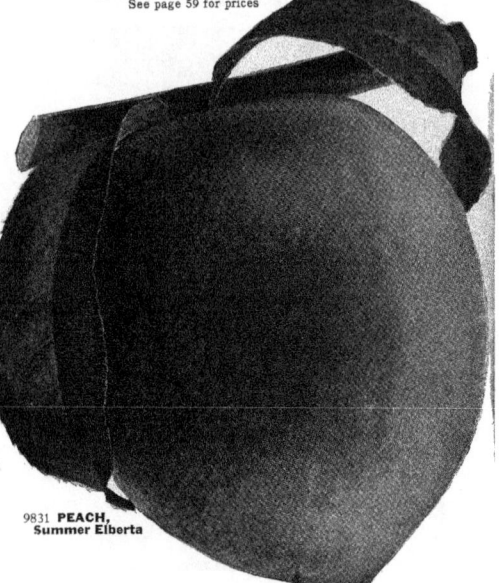

9800
CHERRY, Bing

9800 **BING CHERRY.** A black-red Cherry of exceptionally rich flavor. Bing is wonderfully fruitful and most dependable for home or commercial production. One week earlier than Lambert. Sizes: ⁷⁄₁₆–⁹⁄₁₆, ⁹⁄₁₆–¹¹⁄₁₆, ¹¹⁄₁₆–up.
See page 59 for prices

9831 **PEACH,
Summer Elberta**

62

9966
THOMPSON
SEEDLESS
GRAPE

GRAPES: CONCORD   SENECA   KEUKA

862
PEACH,
H. Hale

P.-W.'s *Delicious*
FRUITS

9976 EVERBEARING RASPBERRY
INDIAN SUMMER
10 for $1.80; 100 for $12.00

9997
NEW EVERBEARING STRAWBERRY
UTAH CENTENNIAL
25 for $2.50; 100 for $7.50

PRINTED
U.S.A.

P.-W's. *Giant Zinnias*

1686 **EXQUISITE**

CPSIA information can be obtained
at www.ICGtesting.com
Printed in the USA
BVHW04s1034210918
528173BV00023B/1747/P